Making Colorful Wire *&* Beaded Jewelry

35 fabulous designs

Making Colorful
Wire &
Beaded
Jewelry

35 fabulous designs

LINDA JONES

INTERWEAVE PRESS
www.interweave.com

This book is dedicated to my wonderful sons, Ben and Charlie; to my parents, who are so constantly supportive; and to my loving and most patient partner, Chris, who has come to understand my complete passion for fiddling with wire and beads!

First edition for North America published in 2006 by Interweave Press LLC.
Copyright © CicoBooks 2006
All inquiries should be addressed to:

Interweave Press LLC
201 East Fourth Street
Loveland, CO 80537
www.interweave.com

Library of Congress Cataloging-in-Publication Data
Jones, Linda.
  Making colorful wire & beaded jewelry : 35 fabulous designs / Linda Jones.
      p. cm.
  Includes index.
  ISBN 1-59668-014-8
 1. Jewelry making. 2. Wire craft. 3. Beadwork. I. Title: Making colorful wire and beaded jewelry. II. Title.
  TT212.J66 2006
  745.594'2--dc22

                              2005028734

Editor: Rebecca Campbell
Technical Editor: Bonnie Brooks
Proofreader: Nancy Arndt

ISBN 1-59668-014-8
Printed in China
10 9 8 7 6 5 4 3 2 1

Contents

Introduction

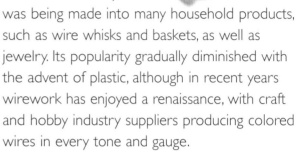

Creating wire jewelry is an ancient craft. Beautiful gold wire necklaces have been discovered in ancient Egyptian burial chambers dating back as far as 3000 BC, and we know that the Assyrians and Babylonians also made wire jewelry around 1700 BC. It is believed that these ancient craftsmen created wire by chiselling thin strips from sheet metal. The strips were either twisted around cylindrical mandrels or rolled between two flat surfaces, such as rocks, to smooth them for use in jewelry.

Today, wire is made by drawing annealed metal rods through shaped holes in a drawplate. The drawplate allows for the manufacture of almost unlimited lengths of wire from any ductile metal. By altering the shape of the drawplate opening, wire can be produced in different shapes, the most common being round. Archaeologists tell us that metal drawplates were used by the Persians in the sixth century BC., as well as in Roman times, and first came to Europe in the tenth century AD, resulting in widespread manufacture of chain-mail armor in medieval times.

The United States imported its wire from the United Kingdom and Germany until 1812, when the war meant that supplies were cut off. From this point, the Americans began building their own

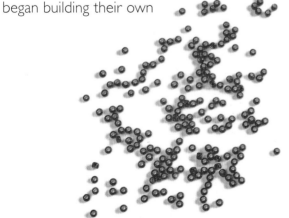

factories for producing wire and by the mid-nineteenth century, wire was being made into many household products, such as wire whisks and baskets, as well as jewelry. Its popularity gradually diminished with the advent of plastic, although in recent years wirework has enjoyed a renaissance, with craft and hobby industry suppliers producing colored wires in every tone and gauge.

If you have never made wire jewelry before, I hope this book will inspire you to pick up a pair of pliers and give it a try! The projects range from ultra-simple designs that are perfect for complete beginners to more elaborate items that you can move on to once you've mastered the basics. Every project is set out like a recipe, with a list of all the "ingredients" you need and clear step-by-step instructions from start to finish. There are flamboyant rings and chokers for the style-conscious trendsetter; delicate chains and accessories for a more classic, understated look; chunky beads that evoke the age-old traditions of Venetian glass or the tribal carvings of East Africa; and brightly colored brooches in vibrant hues of turquoise and fuchsia-pink wire.

I've also included lots of variations to give you some idea of how easy it is to adapt and modify any of the projects to suit your own color combinations and style. Once you gain confidence in using the tools and become familiar with the wire, you will undoubtedly come up with variations of your own. I just hope you will get as much pleasure from making the pieces as I have!

CHAPTER ONE

Tools and Techniques

The joy of making wire and beaded jewelry is that you need very little in the way of special equipment—but when it comes to creating unique, one-of-a-kind pieces, the sky's the limit! From mass-produced plastic to handmade glass beads and semiprecious stones, there are beads in every shape and hue. Wire, too, comes in many colors, from the more traditional copper, silver, and gold to vibrant, almost iridescent shades. Best of all, the techniques really are very simple! Armed with the information in this chapter, you'll be making beautiful, timeless pieces of jewelry of your own design in no time!

Tools

You'll see that you need very little equipment to get started and, most important, most of the equipment is inexpensive. The tools shown on these two pages are nearly everything you will need. Tools and materials can be obtained from large jewelry outlets and craft suppliers. There are also many mail-order catalogs and, of course, the Internet is a great source. For more information on sources, turn to page 126.

Pliers and Cutters

Three types of pliers are used in wire jewelry—round-nose, flat-nose, and chain-nose. You will also need a good pair of wire cutters.

Round-nose pliers have tapered, cone-shaped ends. They are used to coil, curve, and bend wire into small loops or tight curves.

Flat-nose pliers have flat, parallel jaws and are primarily used to grip the wire firmly as you work with it, as

well as to straighten kinks, bend wire at right angles, and flatten loose ends, so that they don't jut out. The difference between flat-nose pliers and general-purpose household pliers is that flat-nose pliers are usually smaller and have no serrations or grips, as this would mark the wire.

Chain-nose pliers are similar to flat-nose pliers, but have tapered ends. They are useful for holding small pieces of wire, or when working on intricate designs.

Wire cutters
There are different kinds of wire cutters on the market, from "shears" to "end cutters," but "side cutters" are the most useful for jewelry making.

A small hammer and steel block— used for flattening and work-hardening wire pieces.

They have small, tapered blades that can cut into small spaces, making them ideal for small-scale work. Invest in a good-quality pair, as the cheaper versions become blunt quite quickly and can squash and distort the cut ends of wire.

Hammer and Flat Steel Block

These tools are used to flatten, spread, and work-harden wire (see page 19). Flat blocks can be obtained from specialty jewelry stores. The steel block must be polished smooth, otherwise your wire will pick up any indentations present on the block.

You can use almost any hammer, provided it is not too heavy and has a polished, smooth, flat steel end. Specialty jewelry hammers are generally smaller and lighter than general-purpose household hammers, and you may find them easier to use.

Mandrel

A mandrel, available from specialty jewelry suppliers, is a tapered, steel cone that is used to form ring shanks and other circular shapes. Mandrels come in various sizes, from small-diameter ones used for making rings to large-scale versions for making

Top: a specialist ring mandrel. Bottom: an improvised mandrel—a wooden dowel bought from a home-improvements store.

From left to right: round-nose pliers, flat-nose pliers, chain-nose pliers, wire cutters.

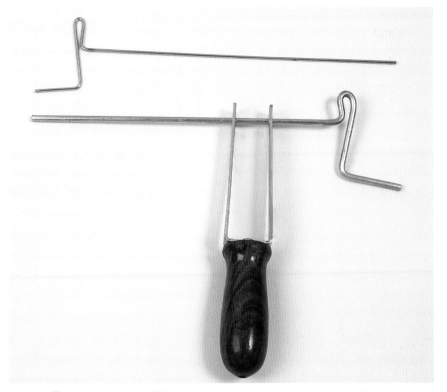

Spiral Bead Maker/Coiling Gizmo

These are manufactured tools that are used for coiling and wrapping lengths of wire.

The Spiral Bead Maker is distributed by The Scientific Wire Company in the U.K. (www.wires.co.uk) and the Coiling Gizmo, invented by LeRoy Goertz, is available in the United States from www.coilinggizmo.com and from many large bead and jewelry suppliers.

Both tools consist of a bracket and two steel handles of different thicknesses. The Spiral Bead Maker has a wooden-handled bracket, while the Coiling Gizmo's bracket can be clamped to a tabletop. The one shown in this book is the Spiral Bead Maker, which can be held by hand. The cranking handle slots into the hole of the bracket and wire is wrapped around the fold of the handle to secure it. The handle is then turned by hand to coil and spiral the wire into long "springs." This tool is useful for making bulk quantities of jump rings, as well as double-spiraled beads, and comes with full instructions.

chokers. They are not essential, as you can improvise by shaping wire around other cylindrical objects of the appropriate size, such as glass jars, wooden dowels, or even knitting needles. If you plan to make lots of rings, however, a ring mandrel is a worthwhile investment as it is marked with gradations showing standard sizes of rings.

A Spiral Bead Maker, with two handles of different thicknesses enabling you to create coils of different diameters.

Hand Drill and Vise

In wire jewelry making, a hand drill is used in conjunction with a vise to twist wires together. Small vises can be bought from any home-improvement store, as well as from large craft suppliers. One end of the wires being twisted is held in the vise, while the other end is fixed in the chuck of the hand drill (see page 17). Again, they are not an essential piece of equipment—but they do make it easier to produce even twists of wire.

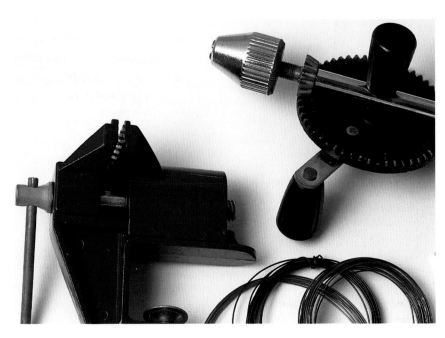

A hand drill and vise—a quick way of twisting wires evenly.

Materials

When it comes to choosing wires and beads for your jewelry, there are so many choices available that you can really let your imagination run wild! Even if you don't have a specific project in mind, you'll probably find yourself storing up materials for use in the future—and once you start, it's totally addictive!

Wire

Wire is available in varying thicknesses, types, and colors. By using different wires on your projects, you can create distinctly different results. Colored, copper, and plated wires can be bought from most craft and hobby stores, as well as from bead suppliers. With the exception of precious metal, wire is generally sold in spools of a pre-measured length.

If you are new to wireworking, it's often difficult to know which wire to purchase. I recommend starting with a general all-purpose 20-gauge (0.8mm) copper wire. Copper is the most flexible wire to use, enabling you to practice and get a feel for shaping and using the pliers, before you embark on silver and gold wire.

Colored wires, which could once be obtained only from electronic industry suppliers, are now widely available in the craft market. Most colored wires are copper based with enamel coatings, which means that they cannot be hammered or over-manipulated, as the surface plating can be removed. However, twisting, coiling, wrapping, and spiraling are all effective techniques.

Once you become confident and proficient in wire jewelry making, you can begin investing in precious-metal wire and create jewelry in sterling silver or 9- or 14-carat gold. Precious-metal wire is obviously more expensive; it is bought by length, the price being calculated by weight. Specialty jewelry outlets supply precious-metal wire in different gauges and shapes—for example, round, half-round, and square.

More unusual kinds of wire for jewelry making include electrical cable, which has a wealth of beautiful copper wires under the plastic outer coating, florist's, and gardening wire. Look around and you'll be surprised at what you can find!

Thicknesses of wire

All these kinds of wire come in different thicknesses, or gauges. The higher the gauge number, the thinner the wire; for example, 20-gauge (0.8mm) wire is thicker than 28-gauge (0.4mm). The most commonly used and general-purpose gauge is 20-gauge (0.8mm). Thicker wires, such as 18-gauge (1mm) and 14-gauge (1.5mm), are used to create more chunky pieces. Thinner wire such as 24-gauge (0.6mm) is useful for threading small-holed beads and delicate general-purpose work, while 28-gauge (0.4mm) is used for fine binding, knitting, or weaving.

Beads

Beads are made from a wide range of materials, including plastic, clay, porcelain, glass, metal, wood, and bone. You don't have to spend a fortune to acquire a collection—local charity and thrift stores are a good, inexpensive source of costume jewelry that you can recycle into your own designs. You can even make your own beads using Fimo, papier mâché, or precious metal clay. Buttons, steel washers, and pre-drilled shells and stones can also be used to create interesting designs.

Copper-, gold-, and silver-plated wires are very versatile and are suitable for both traditional and very contemporary designs, depending on how you choose to embellish them.

Colored wires in a multitude of colors can form the basis for bright, contemporary-looking designs.

Metal beads often have patterns inscribed on them, which gives your jewelry an interesting texture.

Wooden and bone-effect beads can impart a rustic, or ethnic, look to your jewelry pieces.

Glass beads range from completely transparent to almost opaque, and have a quality that is unmatched by any other substance. They can be expensive, so they are perhaps best used as "focal" beads for maximum impact.

Very small beads, known as seed or rocaille beads, are sold in small tubes. Because they are so tiny, you need to string several together for impact.

Findings

"Findings" is the term used to describe ready-made components such as chains, ear wires and clips, key rings, barrettes, pin backs, and so on. They can be purchased from most craft and hobby stores and bead shops. If you are using a ready-made chain, check that the links are large enough to take whatever gauge of wire you used for the embellishment. If the links are not large enough, you may need to make jump rings (see page 16).

Precious-metal findings made from gold and platinum are available from specialty jewelry suppliers.

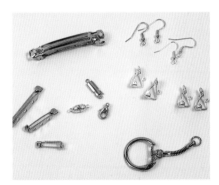

Ready-made findings are widely available in a variety of colors, so it is easy to find one that matches your design.

Organize your beads by color and store them in lidded containers to prevent spillages.

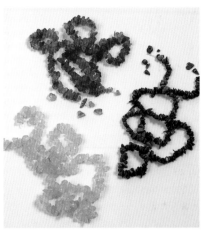

Semiprecious chip stones are sold in 16- or 18-in. (40- or 45-cm) lengths. When you're ready to use them, snip the thread that holds them together and store in small containers. You may be surprised how inexpensive they can be!

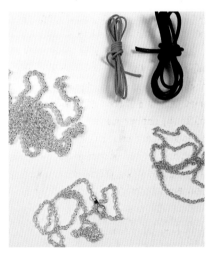

Ready-made chains and cords, on which you can hang your wire embellishments, speed up the process of making a necklace—although you can, of course, make your own chains if you prefer (see page 17).

Basic Techniques

If this is your first attempt at wireworking, I recommend that you read this section thoroughly before you start on any of the projects. Although none of the techniques used in this book is particularly difficult, it is important to master a few basic principles and become familiar with the tools. Practice with inexpensive beads and 20-gauge (0.8mm) copper wire until you feel confident. Copper wire is the most flexible of all types of wire. Once you realize how easy it is to curve, coil, and spiral it, your confidence will improve immeasurably.

Threading Beads with Wire

The basic principle is to construct a neat loop (known as a "link") at each end of the bead, which is then used to connect one bead to another.

STEP 1 Working from the spool, thread your chosen bead onto the wire, leaving about ½" (1cm) of wire extending on each side of the bead.

STEP 2 Remove the bead and snip the wire with the wire cutters.

STEP 3 Thread the bead back onto the cut wire. Holding the wire vertically with the bead in the center, use the tips of your round-nose pliers to bend the wire to a right angle at the point where it touches the bead.

STEP 4 Hold the end of the bent wire tightly with your round-nose pliers and curl it toward you into a circle, shaping it around the shaft of the pliers. It is better to do this in several short movements, repositioning the pliers as necessary, than to attempt to make one continuous circle.

STEP 5 Turn the bead around and form another link at the other side, in exactly the same way.

When you've threaded the bead, make sure the links at each end face in the same direction. Hold one link with flat-nose pliers and the other with round-nose pliers and twist until they both face in the same direction. This will prevent the beads from twisting around when they are linked together as a chain.

Making a Head Pin

If you want to thread a bead with only one suspension link, you will need to make a head pin at one end to prevent the bead from slipping off the wire. You can buy ready-made head pins, but you may find that they are too small for beads with very large holes—so it is a good idea to learn how to make them yourself.

STEP 1 Working from the spool, thread your chosen bead onto the wire, leaving about ¾" (2cm) more wire than the length of your bead.

STEP 2 Using the tips of your round-nose pliers, make a tiny curl at one end of the wire.

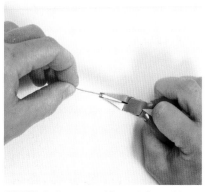

STEP 3 Squeeze this curl flat with your flat-nose pliers to create a knob at one end. (If you've folded too much wire, just snip a little off, ensuring that you don't cut through both doubled wires.)

STEP 4 Slide your bead onto the wire to make sure that it cannot slip off. (If the hole in the bead is large and slips over the head pin, you can use a small seed bead as a stopper or bend the head pin at right angles so that the bead sits on top of it.)

STEP 5 Using your round-nose pliers, curl the other end of the wire into a round link by following Steps 3 and 4 of Threading Beads with Wire, opposite.

The head pin is unobtrusive but prevents the bead from slipping off the wire.

You can also make decorative head pins by leaving a longer length of wire below the bead. From left to right: wire curled into a spiral (page 16); wire hammered so that it spreads into a "feather" shape (page 19); seed bead threaded onto end of wire.

Making Spirals

There are two kinds of spirals—
"open" and "closed."

A closed spiral has no gaps.

An open spiral is made in the same way, but evenly-sized gaps are left between the coils.

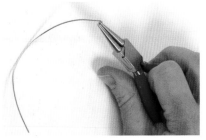

STEP 1 To form a closed spiral, you can either cut a length of wire (as here) or work directly from the spool. Begin by curling a little circle at the end of the wire, using the tips of your round-nose pliers. Make this circle as round as possible, as the rest of the spiral will be shaped around it.

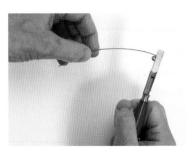

STEP 2 Grip the circle tightly in the jaws of your flat-nose pliers and begin curling the wire around it, making sure that each coil butts up tightly against the previous one.

STEP 3 When the spiral is the size you want, leave about ½" (1cm) of wire to form a suspension loop. Using the tips of your round-nose pliers, curl the projecting end of wire into a small loop in the opposite direction to the spiral.

Making Jump Rings

Jump rings, used to connect units together, are made by constructing a wire spiral, out of which you snip individual coils as required.

When you bring the wire around the pliers to begin forming the second coil, it needs to go below the coil, nearer your hand. This keeps the wire on the same part of the pliers every time. If you bring the wire round above the first coil, the jump rings will taper, following the shape of the pliers' shaft.

STEP 1 Working from the spool, wrap wire five or six times around one shaft of your round-nose pliers, curling it around the same part of the pliers every time to create an even coil.

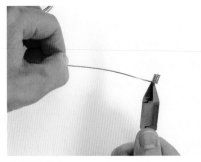

STEP 2 Remove the coil from the pliers and cut it off from the spool of wire with your wire cutters.

STEP 3 Find the cut end and, using your wire cutters, snip upward into the next row of the coil, thereby cutting off a full circle. Continue cutting each coil of the spring in turn to obtain more jump rings.

Using Jump Rings to Connect Units

Using flat-nose pliers, open one of the jump rings sideways (like a door), so that you do not distort the shape. Loop the open jump ring through the links of the beads and close it with flat-nose pliers. The two ends of the jump rings should move just past one another, as the wire will spring back slightly when you remove the pliers. If you don't push the wires hard enough you will end up with a gap, which may mean that the beads will work loose.

Jump rings can be linked together to create a chain. From left to right: silver jump rings linked together; copper jump rings interspersed with pairs of smaller silver jump rings; copper jump rings.

Other ways of forming jump rings

If you find it difficult to keep the wire in the same part of the pliers every time, form the coil by wrapping wire around a small-diameter mandrel, such as a knitting needle or steel rod.

You can also make jump rings using a Spiral Bead Maker or Coiling Gizmo (see page 11). Following the manufacturer's instructions, turn the handle to create long "springs" of wire, then cut off individual coils when you need them, just as you would with normal jump rings.

Twisting Wires Together

I recommend using a vise and hand drill for this technique, as it is both quick and effective. If you do not have these tools, however, attach one end of your wires to a door handle or nail and the other to a wooden handle such as a wooden spoon and, keeping the wires straight and taut, twist them in the same direction until you achieve the effect you want.

Always twist wires of the same thickness. If you end up with an uneven twist or bumps in your wire, it just means that some of the wires were longer or looser than others!

Cut two lengths of 20-gauge (0.8mm) wire and bind the ends with masking tape. Place one end in the chuck of the hand drill and the other end in the vise. Hold the hand drill, so that the wires are straight and taut, and gently turn the handle in one direction. (Do not twist too much or the wires will lose flexibility and become weak and brittle.) When the twist is complete, remove the wires from the chuck of the hand drill and from the vise and snip off the taped ends.

Fish-hook Clasp

Many clasps are available ready made from craft and bead suppliers. However, a beautiful piece of jewelry can be ruined by the inclusion of a clasp that doesn't match. Making your own clasps also gives you the opportunity to experiment with different shapes.

The most commonly used clasp is the "Fish Hook," which is also one of the simplest to create.

Fish-hook Clasp

STEP 1 Working from the spool, curl the end of the wire into a small loop using the tips of your round-nose pliers. Reposition your pliers on the other side of the wire, just under the loop, and curl the wire in the opposite direction around the wider part of the pliers to form the fish-hook clasp.

STEP 2 Cut the wire off the spool, leaving about ½" (1cm) to create a link (see page 14). If you wish, you can gently hammer the hook to work-harden and flatten it slightly, thereby making it stronger and more durable.

The "Eye" of the Fish-hook Clasp

STEP 1 Curl a piece of 20-gauge (0.8mm) wire around the widest part of your round-nose pliers about 1" (2.5cm) from the end of the wire, crossing the end of the wire over itself.

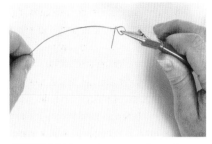

STEP 2 Wrap the extending wire around the stem, just under the circle.

STEP 3 Cut the wire off the spool, leaving about ½" (1cm) extending, and curl this into a link using your round-nose pliers (see page 14).

STEP 4 Gently hammer the top curve of the "eye" to toughen and flatten it. Do not hammer the wires that have been wrapped over the stem, or you will weaken them.

The completed hook and eye can be linked to the ends of a necklace or bracelet chain, either directly or via jump rings.

Hammering flattens and toughens the clasp.

Basic S-hook Clasp

An S-shaped clasp is another popular decorative clasp.

STEP 1 Working from the spool, curl a tiny loop at the end of the wire with your round-nose pliers. Place the widest part of your pliers just under the loop and curve the wire in the opposite direction.

STEP 2 Cut the wire off the spool, turn the piece over, and make a small loop at the other end of the wire.

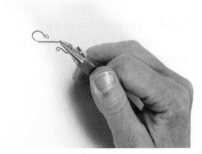

STEP 3 Place the widest part of your pliers just under the loop and curve the wire in the opposite direction to create a mirror image to the first curve and complete the "S" shape.

Beaded S-hook

As a variation on the basic S-hook, incorporate a bead in the center of the clasp.

STEP 1 Make the first curve of the S-Hook, following the instructions for Step 1 of the Basic S-Hook Clasp. Cut the wire to the desired length and thread on a small bead.

STEP 2 Follow Steps 2 and 3 of the Basic S-Hook Clasp to complete the S-shape.

STEP 3 Wrap a finer-gauge of wire around the clasp on either side of the bead to hold it in place.

A bead makes a pretty finishing touch for the clasp. Choose a bead that complements those used in the main piece.

Understanding Work Hardening

There's nothing more disheartening than spending time creating a lovely piece of jewelry only to have it fall apart or break once you've worn it a few times. To create functional wire jewelry without the aid of solder, you must know how to work-harden, or toughen, your material so that it can take the strain of being worn without distorting and falling apart.

Most of the wire that you buy is pre-annealed, which means that it is soft and flexible to work with. When it is toughened through manipulation, the compression changes that occur in its crystal structure provide it with rigidity, which results in a more solid, functional piece. If you overwork it, wire loses its malleability, causing fractures to occur where it is most stressed; the wire will eventually become so weak and brittle that it will break.

In traditional jewelry making it is possible to return wire or metal to a malleable state by heating or annealing the wire, rendering it flexible and workable again. To explain the process of work hardening, I suggest you cut a small length of wire (say 2"/5cm of 20-gauge/0.8mm), hold one end tightly with your fingers, and the other end with a pair of round-nose pliers. Now gently twist the wire around, holding it straight and taut. As you do so, you should be able to feel it toughening and strengthening. There is a comfortable point where it is hard (or work hardened) and strong enough to use in a piece of jewelry—but if you twist the wire or metal too much, it will become brittle and weak and will eventually break.

Another effective way of work-hardening metal is to hammer it on a steel block. The block must be clean, smooth, and dent-free, or the wire will pick up irregularities. To practice hammering, make a wiggled wire shape or spiral. Place this shape on your steel block and "stroke" hammer it, ensuring the flat part of the hammer comes down at 90 degrees to the piece. It is easiest to hammer your piece standing up, as this ensures that the hammer head hits the wire squarely, rather than at an angle, which could create texturing and "dimples" in the metal. After hammering the piece several times on each side, you should notice the wire flattening, spreading, and work-hardening. It is important to note that this technique is not suitable for colored wires, as the colored coatings can rub off, or for small jump rings and links, as it will distort their shape.

To strengthen a jump ring, take one end in your round-nose pliers and the other in your chain-nose pliers and gently push them just past the point at which they should join. When you've done this two or three times, the ends should want to spring back together; the piece will be work-hardened just enough to hold the join without the aid of solder.

Through practice and experience, you will get a "feel" for the metal and understand how much stress and tempering you can use.

Stroking, or rubbing, the wire with the head of the hammer also toughens and strengthens the wire. This is often referred to as "burnishing."

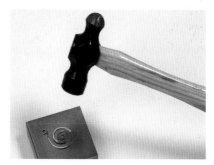

Hammering a piece of wire on a steel block tempers and flattens the wire.

CHAPTER TWO

Rings and Things

The projects in this chapter are all relatively small and simple to make but, if you're new to wire jewelry, they will give you a good grounding in all the basic techniques. At the same time, you will create attractive, unique pieces that make perfect gifts for family and friends.

Squiggle Ring

Squiggles of wire, achieved simply by bending the wire around your pliers, make up the top of this modern-looking ring. The irregular sizes and angles of the bends are part of the design's charm, so don't worry about making it look symmetrical! It's very quick to make, as it's all created from one continuous piece of wire. You can use colored or plated wire, sterling silver or gold, for this project. Practice with copper wire, just to build up your confidence; once you've mastered the technique, you'll be ready to make one in 14-carat gold!

MATERIALS
- 12–14" (30–35cm) 20-gauge (0.8mm) wire
- 1 decorative 4mm bead

TOOLS
- Round- and flat-nose pliers
- Wire cutters
- Mandrel or dowel

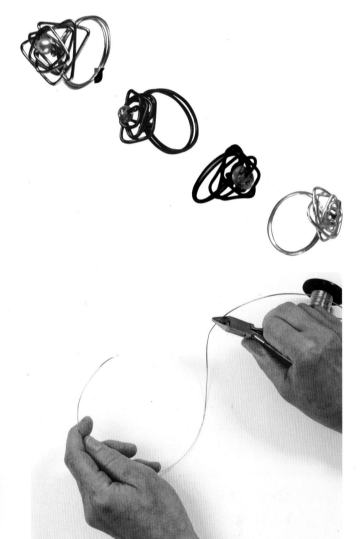

VARIATION: Colored Squiggles

Colored wire makes a fun and funky alternative to the gold wire shown in the demonstration. Choose a focal bead that stands out well, such as a clear bead against jet black wire, or a metallic bead against bright red.

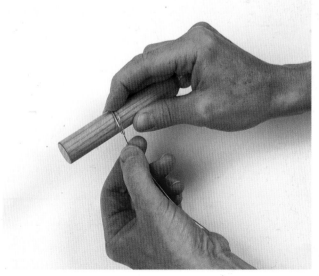

STEP 1 Cut a 12–14-in. (30–35-cm) length of 20-gauge (0.8mm) wire.

STEP 2 Wrap the wire a couple of times tightly around a mandrel to shape the shank of the ring. If you don't have a mandrel, use a dowel that is slightly smaller in diameter than you want the finished ring shank to be.

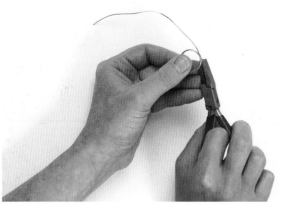

STEP 3 Secure the cut end of the wire by wrapping it around the circular shank two or three times, leaving at least 5–6" (12–15cm) of wire extending. Use your flat-nose pliers to press the wire tightly against the shank.

STEP 4 Hold the end of the extended wire with your flat-nose pliers and bend it in small, random angles.

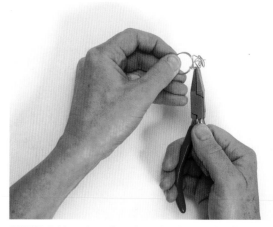

STEP 5 Increase the size of the bends in the wire as you get closer to the shank of the ring.

STEP 6 Keep bending the wire in angular folds until it sits directly against the ring shank.

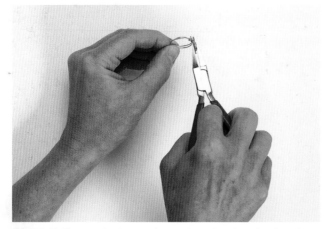

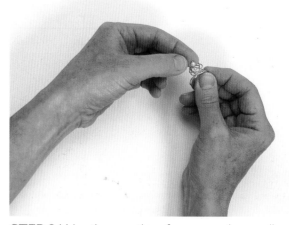

STEP 7 Flatten the bent wire against the ring shank with your flat-nose pliers and spend a little time rearranging it into a shape that you like by twisting the wire around with your pliers to expose the layers underneath.

STEP 8 Using the very tips of your round-nose pliers, pull the central end wire out of the squiggle. Then thread a small focal bead onto it.

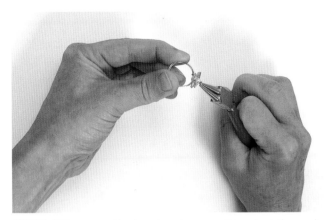

STEP 9 To secure the bead, make a small hook at the end of the wire using the tips of your round-nose pliers.

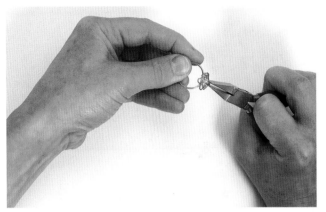

STEP 10 Squash the hook flat with the ends of your flat-nose pliers to create a knob of wire. This forms a head pin (see page 15), which will prevent the bead from slipping off the wire. Spend a little extra time rearranging the front of the ring until you are satisfied with the centerpiece.

VARIATION: Beadless Squiggles

You can also make squiggle rings entirely from wire, without any focal bead in the center. To do this, form the ring shank, as described in Steps 1 through 3, and then form a spiral (see page 16) or wiggly shape for the top of the ring. Complete the ring by bending the wire at random angles until it sits snugly against the ring shank.

Framed-bead Key Ring

This project is perfect for highlighting a single, beautiful bead. Simply increase or reduce the amount of wire that you use for the "frame" to suit the size and shape of your bead. You could use the same technique to make a pendant or, if you have two identical beads, earrings.

STEP 1 Take a dowel slightly wider in diameter than the bead you wish to frame. Pulling the silver wire out from the spool, wrap it around the dowel until one piece passes over the other. Cut the wire off the spool, leaving about ½" (1cm) on each side of the circle of wire.

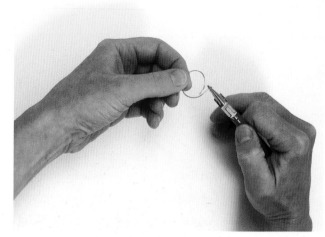

STEP 2 Using your round-nose pliers, curl one end of the wire into a small loop (see page 14).

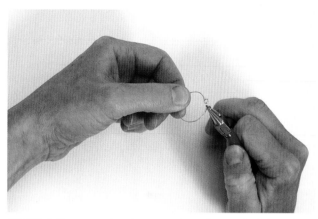

STEP 3 Form another loop on the other end of the wire, making sure that the two loops curl away from each other.

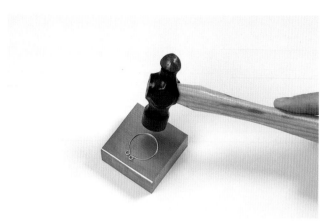

STEP 4 Place the wire on a steel block and gently hammer the curve of the frame, avoiding the loops at the top. The metal at the base of the piece will spread; hammering also tempers and hardens the metal (see page 19).

STEP 5 Using your flat-nose pliers, twist the top loops 90°, so that they face each other.

STEP 6 Thread the focal bead onto a short length of 20-gauge (0.8mm) wire and form a head pin at one end and a link at the other (see page 15).

VARIATION: Oval Bead Frame

To make a frame for an oval-shaped bead, wrap the wire around the dowel as before, but cut the wire off the spool when you have formed a complete circle (in other words, without leaving an overlap on each side). Follow Steps 2 and 3 to form the loops on each side and bring these loops together, thereby foreshortening the circle, creating an oval or elongated frame. Follow Steps 4 through 8 and suspend an oval bead within the frame to create an attractive necklace design.

STEP 7 Make a large jump ring (see page 16). Thread the jump ring through one of the top loops of the frame, then through the link of the feature bead, and finally through the second top loop of the frame, thereby suspending the bead in the center of the frame.

STEP 8 Connect the framed-bead unit to a ready-made key-ring finding, opening and closing the jump ring at the top of the frame with your flat-nose pliers.

VARIATION: ## Beaded Color Frame

For a more colorful effect, thread small seed beads onto the wire frame. Omit Step 4 (the hammering)—otherwise you will shatter the beads!

Curly-wurly Brooch

Although this looks like quite a complicated piece, all you have to do is thread lengths of contrasting-colored wire onto a ready-made pin back and spiral the ends. The beads are held in place by the spirals so, if you're new to wire jewelry and don't feel entirely confident about your ability to make links and head pins, this is a great project to start with. To make a bigger brooch, use longer wires; for a bolder, chunkier effect, use more wires than suggested.

MATERIALS
- 21" (52.5cm) 24-gauge (0.6mm) pink wire
- 20" (50cm) 24-gauge (0.6mm) purple wire
- 4–6 silver beads, approx. 4–6mm in diameter
- Ready-made pin back, approx. 1½" (4cm) long, with 3 holes

TOOLS
- Round- and flat-nose pliers
- Wire cutters

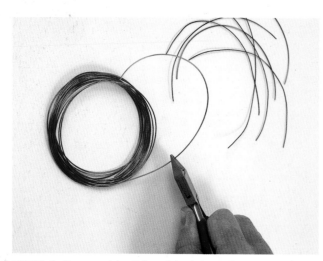

STEP 1 Cut one 6-in. (15-cm) and three 5-in. (12.5-cm) lengths of pink wire and four 5-in. (12.5-cm) lengths of purple wire.

STEP 2 Thread the 6-in. (15-cm) length through the first hole of the pin back from the front and bring it back up again through the third hole.

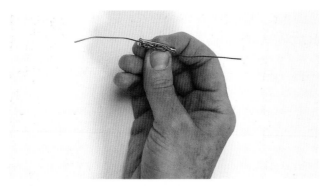

STEP 3 Flatten the wire tightly against the back of the pin back by squeezing it with your flat-nose pliers. Bring the two wires together at the front and twist them together to secure, leaving one end of wire extending on each side of the pin back. Don't twist too much or you will weaken the wire and it will snap.

STEP 4 Thread a small bead onto each extending wire at the front to cover the twist and push it down as far as it will go.

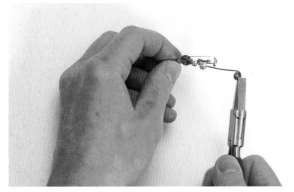

STEP 5 Using your round-nose pliers, make a small loop at the end of each wire. Then, holding the loop securely with your flat-nose pliers, curl the rest of the wire around the loop to form a spiral (see page 16). Work the spiral right up to the bead.

STEP 6 Once you have made the first two spirals, thread the 5-in. (12.5-cm) lengths of wire in between (and underneath the first twist). Add beads to some of the wires, as in Step 4, then spiral the ends in the same way.

STEP 7 Continue threading the wires by pushing them underneath the first twist and securing. Curl the ends of the wires into tight and "open" spirals to give variety to the front of your brooch.

STEP 8 When you have used up all the wires, spend a little time manipulating the spirals into a pleasing pattern with your fingers, making sure that the pin back is hidden. If the wires feel loose, just twist and secure the spirals and beads over each other. If you want a fuller effect, you can always add more wire and beads.

VARIATIONS: Curly-wurly Chic

Combine different colors of wire for different effects—bright blues and turquoises for a funky,
modern look; silver wire with gold and pearl beads for a more understated, classic effect; or
silver and black for a contemporary, modernist feel.

Scarf Ring

This is a really fun way of holding a scarf in place. You could also use it as a belt buckle or to secure a beach sarong. I've used silver and copper wires—but you could choose wires to complement the colors of your scarf if you prefer.

To use the scarf ring, thread both ends of your scarf down through the top circle, under the central spiral, and back up through the bottom circle. Slide the scarf ring up to the desired position; the "buckle" will hold the scarf neatly together.

MATERIALS
- 16" (40cm) 20-gauge (0.8mm) silver wire
- 16" (40cm) 20-gauge (0.8mm) copper wire

TOOLS
- Mandrel or dowel about 1" (25mm) in diameter
- Masking tape
- Round- and flat-nose pliers
- Wire cutters
- Hand drill
- Table vise

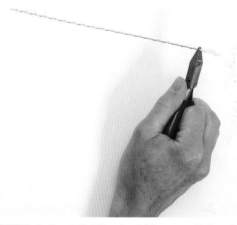

STEP 1 Cut 16" (40cm) of 20-gauge (0.8mm) silver wire and 16" (40cm) of 20-gauge (0.8mm) copper wire. Bind the ends together with masking tape and straighten. Place one end in the table vise and the other in the chuck of the hand drill, and slowly turn the drill handle, keeping the wires taut to prevent any kinks from developing (see page 17). Once the wires have twisted evenly, remove from the drill and vise and cut off the taped ends.

STEP 2 Place the center of your twisted wire around the mandrel or dowel and wrap it around to form a circle.

STEP 3 Turn the wire over and curl the other end around the mandrel in the opposite direction, creating a figure-eight shape.

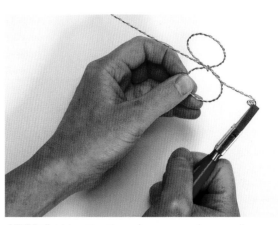

STEP 4 With your flat-nose pliers, pick up one of the loose ends of wire and wrap it over the inner part of both circles a couple of times to hold the piece together as a

STEP 5 Using the tips of your round-nose pliers, curl a small circle at the end of one of the twisted wires.

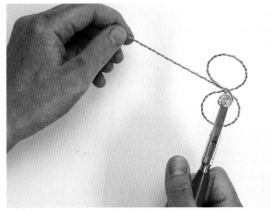

STEP 6 Grip the small circle of wire very firmly with your flat-nose pliers and continue curling the wire around itself to form a spiral.

STEP 7 Repeat Steps 5 and 6 to create another spiral of wire on the other loose end of wire. Spend a little time positioning the spirals in the center of each side. To work-harden or toughen the piece, you could gently "stroke" hammer it on a steel block, but this is not essential.

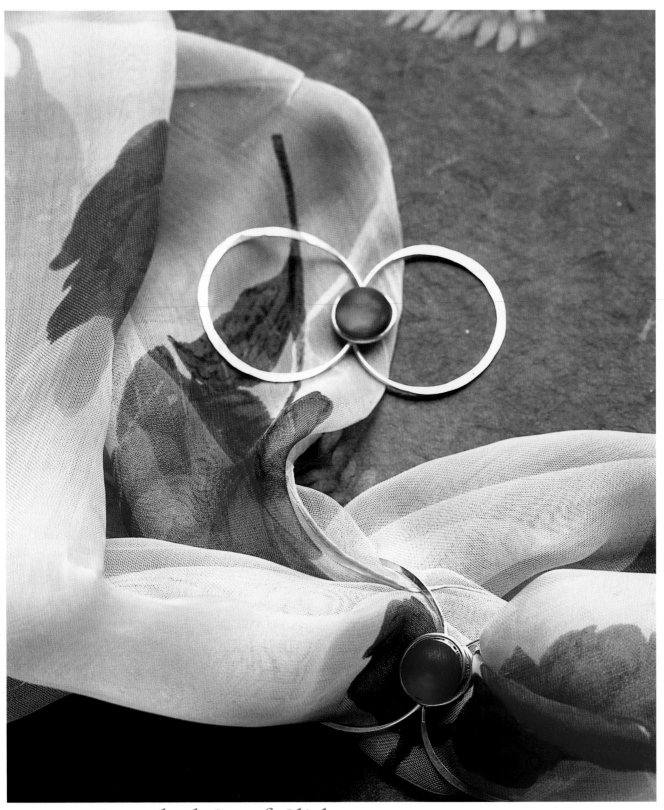

VARIATION: Jeweled Scarf Slide

Instead of twisting colored wires together, you could fabricate the scarf slide from a single piece of wire, such as 18-gauge (1mm) silver wire. Add a spot of color by gluing a cabochon to the center of the spiral.

CHAPTER THREE

Decorative Chainmaking

Once you know how to link one unit to another, you'll find that there is virtually no limit to the styles of chain that can be created with wire. This chapter contains a range of chain designs, from coiled spirals and simple twists of wire to daisy-shaped units and loops. Any or all are sure to inspire you to come up with your own designs!

Bubble-chain Bracelet

This charming bracelet is constructed from "bubbles" of silver wire, made by coiling the wire around the tip of your pliers—a simple technique, but one that looks very effective. Don't worry if the chain units differ slightly from each other. This simply adds to the charm and originality of the piece. If you want to make a chunkier, heavier chain, wrap thicker-gauge wire around a cylindrical mandrel.

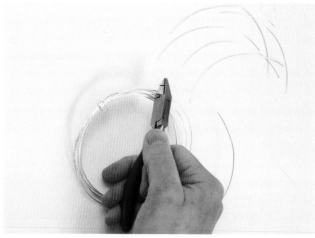

MATERIALS
- 28" (70cm) 20-gauge (0.8mm) silver or gold wire

TOOLS
- Round- and flat-nose pliers
- Wire cutters

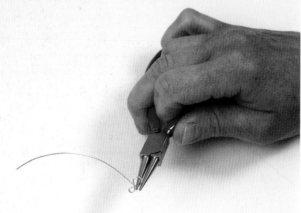

STEP 1 To make a bracelet about 7" (18cm) long, cut seven 4-in. (10-cm) lengths of 20-gauge (0.8mm) wire.

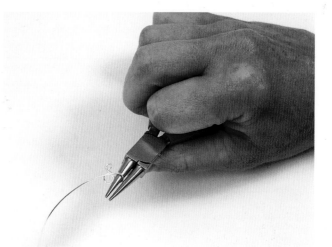

STEP 2 Take the first length of wire and, using your round-nose pliers, curl a small loop at one end. Place the pliers just under this first loop and wrap the wire around the shaft to create a slightly larger circle just below the first one.

STEP 3 Curl the wire around the shaft of the pliers in the opposite direction to form another circle, just below the previous one.

STEP 4 Continue in this way, wrapping the wire around the pliers in the opposite direction each time, until you have made a total of six circles.

STEP 5 Complete the unit by curling a small loop at the end of the wire, using your round-nose pliers. Repeat Steps 2 through 5 to create five more bubble-chain units.

STEP 6 Straighten each bubble-chain unit by squeezing it flat between the jaws of your flat-nose pliers.

STEP 7 Using the tips of your round-nose pliers, make a small loop at the end of the remaining piece of wire.

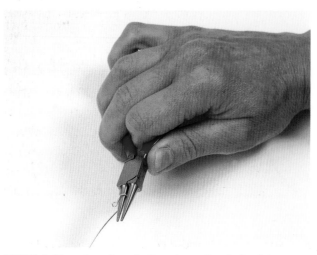

STEP 8 Place the pliers farther down the shaft of the pliers, where the diameter is greater, and curl the wire in the opposite direction to form a hook.

STEP 9 Following Steps 2 and 3, continue curling the wire around the shaft of the pliers just below the hook to form more "bubbles."

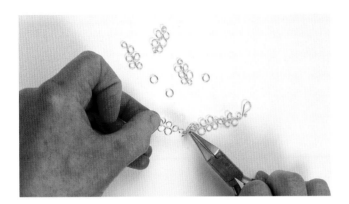

STEP 10 Make jump rings (see page 16) and connect all of the units together to complete the bracelet, making sure that the hook is at the end.

VARIATION: Beaded Bubbles

Make a necklace that matches the color of your outfit by interspersing pastel-colored threaded beads between the bubble-chain units. To make matching earrings, follow Steps 2 through 7 of the bracelet. Make two bubble-chain units, connect them to ready-made ear wires, and suspend a threaded bead (see page 14) from the last "bubble" of each unit. If you want just a tiny dot of color, thread a couple of very small beads onto the jump rings that link the chain units together.

Eyeglasses Chain

If you're continually putting your eyeglasses down and forgetting where you've left them, then this is the project for you! The metal "beads" in the chain are actually tightly coiled spirals of colored wire. Enamel-coated wires are readily available in every tone and shade—so you can be as bold and colorful as you like!

The instructions given here make a chain about 22–24" (55–60cm) long. To make a longer or shorter chain, increase or decrease the number of coils and stick-twist chain units.

MATERIALS

- Approx. 10' (3m) 24-gauge (0.6mm) colored wire
- 24" (60cm) 20-gauge (0.8mm) silver wire
- 18" (45cm) 18-gauge (1mm) silver wire
- Eyeglasses connector findings

TOOLS

- Spiral Bead Maker or Coiling Gizmo
- Round- and flat-nose pliers
- Wire cutters
- Hammer and steel block

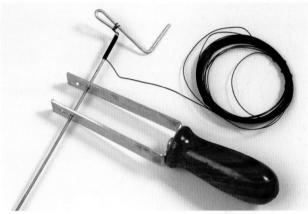

STEP 1 Following the instructions on your Spiral Bead Maker or Coiling Gizmo, make long coils of colored wire, keeping the wire tightly spiraled together.

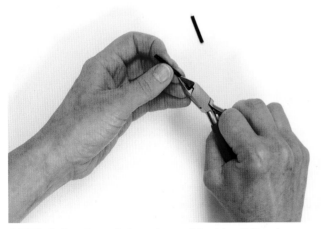

STEP 2 Cut the coils into about eight 1-in. (2.5-cm) lengths and snip off any spiky bits to neaten the ends.

STEP 3 Thread each coil with 20-gauge (0.8mm) silver wire, just as you would thread a bead (see page 14), and form a link at each end of each coil.

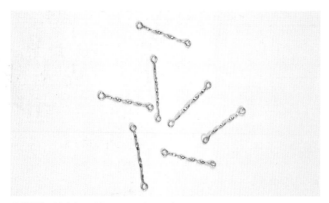

STEP 4 Using 18-gauge (1mm) silver wire, make seven stick-twist chain units (see pages 51–52).

STEP 5 Using your round-nose pliers, make 14 jump rings (see page 16) and connect all the units in a long chain, alternating colored coils and silver stick-twist units. To complete, attach an eyeglasses connector finding to each end of the chain with jump rings, using your flat-nose pliers.

VARIATIONS: Beaded Eyeglasses Chains

These variations do not contain the stick-twist chains. Make the coils from silver wire and thread a colored bead at each end (top). Alternatively, create coils of colored wire using your Spiral Bead Maker or Coiling Gizmo and spiral these colored coils into wire beads. These can then be threaded and linked into an eyeglasses chain, interspersed with silver beads.

Looped Bead Earrings

These earrings can be made in various sizes simply by altering the length of the wire spirals and the size of the bead in the center. As wires are available in a wide range of colors, you can match them to almost any outfit. For a really dramatic statement, you could even create two colored spirals, one suspended within the other!

MATERIALS
- 5' (1.2m) 24-gauge (0.6mm) black wire
- 12" (30cm) 20-gauge (0.8mm) silver wire
- 1 pair ear wires
- 2 black oval 6mm beads

TOOLS
- Spiral Bead Maker or Coiling Gizmo (optional)
- Round- and flat-nose pliers
- Wire cutters
- Mandrel or dowel

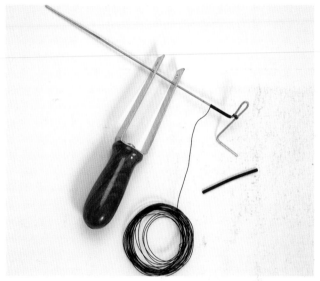

STEP 1 Using a Spiral Bead Maker or Coiling Gizmo, or following the instructions on page 16, spiral about 2½" (6–7cm) of 24-gauge (0.6mm) black wire for each earring.

STEP 2 Cut two 3¼-in. (8.25-cm) lengths of 20-gauge (0.8mm) silver wire and curve each one into a U-shape by bending it around a mandrel or dowel.

STEP 3 Feed a black spiral onto each curved silver wire. Using round-nose pliers, make a link at each end of the curved silver wires (see page 14).

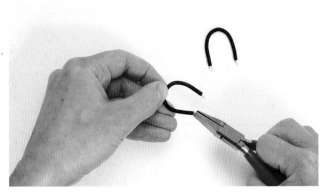

STEP 4 Using flat-nose pliers, twist the links at 90° so that they face each other.

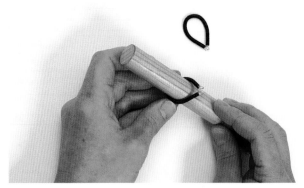

STEP 5 Mold the looped frames around the mandrel or dowel to re-shape them, making sure that the top links sit close together.

STEP 6 Thread the black beads onto 20-gauge (0.8mm) silver wire and make a link at each end (see page 14).

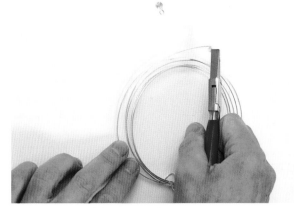

STEP 7 Using 20-gauge (0.8mm) silver wire, make two small, tight spirals (see page 16). Make a link at one end of each spiral and connect one spiral to each bead.

STEP 8 Make two large jump rings from 20-gauge (0.8mm) silver wire (see page 16), and thread them through the links at the top of each earring, suspending the bead in the center.

STEP 9 To complete the earrings, connect them to ready-made ear wires.

Stick-twist Chain

This delicate-looking chain, with alternating twists of gold and silver wire, suits being created as a long piece, as the twisted units extend and stretch out without much articulation. It could also be used as an eyeglasses chain. The instructions given here are for a chain about 18" (45cm) long.

MATERIALS
- 24" (60cm) 20-gauge (0.8mm) silver wire
- 24" (60cm) 20-gauge (0.8mm) gold wire

TOOLS
- Round-, chain-, and flat-nose pliers
- Wire cutters
- Hammer and steel block

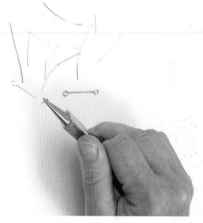

STEP 1 Cut fourteen 1½-in. (4-cm) lengths of wire, seven each of gold and silver. Using round-nose pliers, make a link at each end of each wire (see page 14). Using flat-nose pliers, carefully straighten the wire out at the center of each unit.

VARIATION: Earrings

You can make matching earrings using three of the stick-twist units, with beads threaded onto the ends, suspended in varying lengths, and connected to ready-made ear wires.

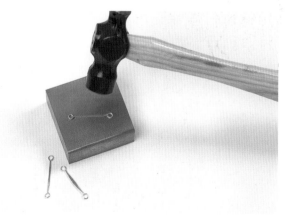

STEP 2 Gently hammer the stem of each unit on a steel block, avoiding the links at the ends. This will flatten and spread the wire in the center of the unit—but make sure you don't hit your fingers!

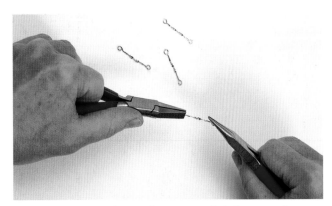

STEP 3 Using both your flat-nose and chain-nose pliers, firmly grip the links at each end of the unit. Twist both pliers around two or three times, making sure that the links finish facing in the same direction. (Be careful not to over twist, as you will weaken the units just under the links and they will break off.)

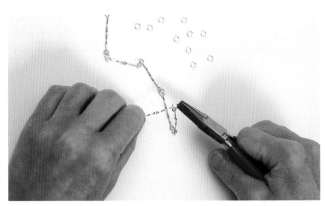

STEP 4 From silver wire, make jump rings (see page 16) and connect all the twisted units together to form a chain.

STEP 5 Curl a tiny loop at the end of a spool of silver wire. Place the widest part of your round-nose pliers just under this loop and curl the wire in the opposite direction to form a hook shape about 1" (2.5cm) long. Cut the wire off the spool, leaving about ½" (1cm), and make a link at the end (see page 14) so that you can connect the fish-hook clasp to the end of the chain.

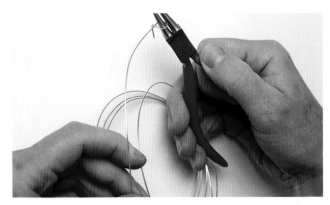

STEP 6 To make the eye of the clasp, wrap the wire around the widest part of your round-nose pliers, crossing the ends over near the base of the circle.

STEP 7 Wrap the end of the crossed-over wire around the stem to secure.

STEP 8 Cut the wire off the spool, leaving about ½" (1cm) at the end to make a link (see page 18). Connect the fish-hook clasp and eye to the ends of the chain.

VARIATION: Beaded Stick-twist Chain

For a more ornate and decorative finish, try suspending threaded beads between the stick-twist units—a great option if you want to match the chain to the colors in a favorite dress or outfit. A silver stick-twist chain paired with bright red beads, as shown here, is a classy combination. Alternatively, suspend some beads from the connecting jump rings so that they hang down and "dance" off the chain. This variation is extremely effective on a bracelet or anklet.

Daisy Chain Bracelet

Definitely a design for the young at heart, this daisy chain looks
fantastic in vibrant colors such as fuchsia or turquoise. Make up
your own variations, perhaps alternating daisies in two or three complementary colors or
threading beads in between the flowers. Individual flowers also look great on the front of
homemade cards or sewn onto cloth bags and straw summer hats. To make smaller flowers,
just use a thinner gauge of wire.

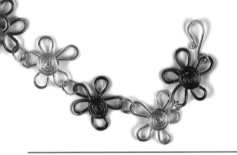

> ### MATERIALS
> - 24–36" (60–90cm) 20-gauge (0.8mm) colored wire
> - 24–36" (60–90cm) 20-gauge (0.8mm) silver wire
> ### TOOLS
> - Round- and flat-nose pliers
> - Wire cutters

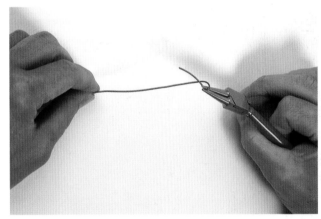

STEP 1 Working directly from the spool, form a loop
around the shaft of your round-nosed pliers about 1"
(2.5cm) from the end of the wire.

VARIATION: Matching Set

You can make a complete set of matching daisy jewelry in
any color combination of your choice. For earrings, make
two daisy units from each color of wire, following Steps 1
through 6 of the Daisy Chain, and suspend each pair from
ready-made ear wires. If you wish, you can attach a wire
spiral or bead to the base petal for added decoration. For
stud earrings, glue flat stud backs to the back of your pieces.
To make a matching ring, follow Steps 1 through 4 of the
Cascade Ring on page 102 and wire a daisy unit to the top.

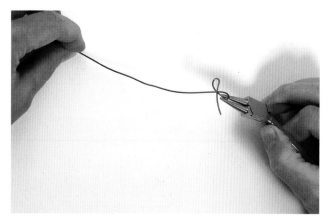

STEP 2 Cross the wire over the first loop and make a second loop, opposite the first one.

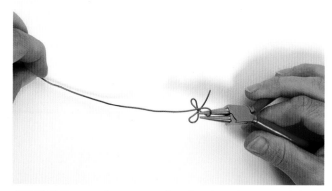

STEP 3 Repeat the process, looping the wire around the pliers so that the loops sit opposite each other.

STEP 4 Continue forming loops until you have 5 or 6 "petals." Cut the wire off the spool, leaving 1–2" (2.5–5cm) extending. Turn the daisy over and wrap the short end of wire (left from making the first loop) around the center of the flower and secure. Cut off any excess and squeeze the flower flat with your flat-nose pliers.

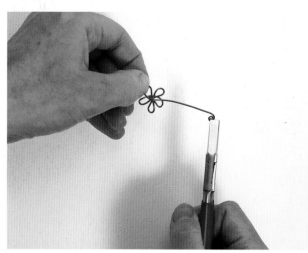

STEP 5 Using the tips of your round-nose pliers, curl a circle at the end of the extended wire. Press this circle tightly with your flat-nose pliers and spiral the wire until it reaches the center of the daisy.

STEP 6 Hold the spiral with your flat-nose pliers and fold it over so that it sits in the center of the flower and hides all the criss-crossing wires. Spend a little time straightening and flattening the petals and adjusting the overall shape of the daisy with your fingers or flat-nose pliers. Repeat Steps 1 through 6 to make six more daisy units, half in colored wire and half in silver.

STEP 7 Make jump rings from 20-gauge (0.8mm) silver wire and connect all the flowers together in a chain, alternating colored and silver daisies and making sure that all the daisy units face the same way (see page 14).

STEP 8 Make a fish-hook clasp (see page 17) and connect it to one end of the daisy chain. There is no need to make an eye for the clasp, as the hook simply hooks over one of the daisy petals.

VARIATION: Silver Daisy Necklace

For a more classic, understated look, make an odd number of daisy units from silver wire and attach them to the center of a ready-made silver chain, spacing them evenly.

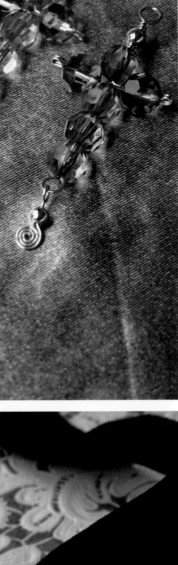

CHAPTER FOUR

Chokers and Necklaces

A distinctive necklace is always a conversation starter, especially if you can say you made it yourself. One of the advantages of making your own jewelry is that you can match the style and colors to your outfits.

In this chapter you will find a range of designs to suit all ages and tastes, including a choker band made from twisted colored wire, a simple cross of brightly colored beads, and a highly contemporary piece made by recycling small pieces of broken chain. Use this chapter to create your own conversation starter!

Spiral Choker

Vibrant turquoise and green wires, reminiscent of peacock feathers, are twisted together to form the ring of this choker, with spirals of the same colors creating the centerpiece. Use a combination of tight and more open spirals to give the piece a sense of airiness.

For a more classic look, try combining gold and silver wires. Increase or reduce the amount of wire that you spiral to suit your own taste. This is one of those designs that evolves and grows as you create it; it can never look the same way twice!

MATERIALS

- Three tones of 24-gauge (0.6mm) wire, approx. 5' (1.5m) of each

TOOLS

- Masking tape
- Round- and flat-nose pliers
- Wire cutters
- Hand drill
- Table vise
- Hammer and steel block

STEP 1 Cut three 20-in. (50-cm) lengths of 24-gauge (0.6mm) wire, one from each color of wire. Bind the ends together with masking tape and straighten. Place one taped end in the table vise and the other in the chuck of the hand drill, and slowly turn the drill handle, keeping all wires taut to avoid any kinks from developing (see page 17). Once all the wires have twisted evenly, remove from the drill and vise and cut off the taped ends.

STEP 2 Unravel approximately 1½" (4cm) at one end of the twist and separate all the wires. Wrap two of the three wires around the twisted stem a couple of times to secure. Snip off any spiky ends.

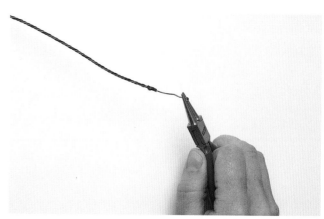

STEP 3 Using your round-nose pliers, curl the end of the remaining wire into a small loop.

STEP 4 Create a second, much larger, loop by curling the wire in the opposite direction, just under the first circle, to complete the fish-hook fastener.

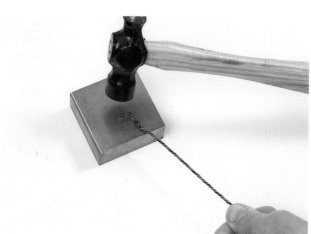

STEP 5 Hammer the end of the fish hook to flatten and work-harden it—but do not hammer any of the wrapped wires or they will become weak and brittle.

STEP 6 To form the eye of the fastener, unravel the wires on the opposite end of the twist, as in Step 2, and separate them out. Wrap two of the wires around the stem of the twist, until you are left with just one wire protruding. Bend this wire at right angles and then form a loop around your round-nose pliers, with the end overlapping the stem. Secure by wrapping it around the stem a couple of times. Cut off any excess. Hammer the end of the loop, as in Step 5, to work-harden it.

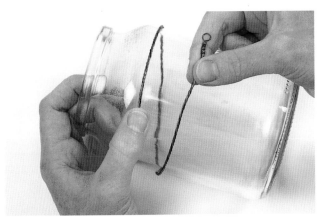

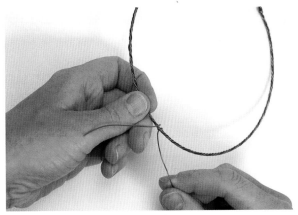

STEP 7 To create the circular shape of the choker, find a cylindrical object about 4" (10cm) in diameter (such as a bottle or cookie jar) and wrap the twisted wires around it tightly, overlapping the ends.

STEP 8 Cut 10–15 pieces of 24-gauge (0.6mm) colored wire, 6–8" (15–20cm) in length. Cut roughly the same number of pieces from each of your three colors of wire. Find the center of the choker ring and wrap the center of the first wire around the frame a couple of times, leaving both ends sticking out.

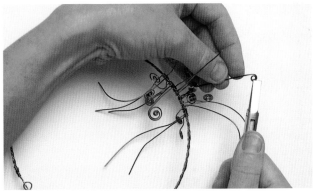

STEP 9 Continue until you have used up all the wires, making sure that they are centered on the front of the choker ring.

STEP 10 Using flat-nose pliers, curl the ends of the wires in concentric circles to make spirals (see page 16), leaving a small gap between the spirals and the choker frame. Make both open and closed spirals.

STEP 11 Spend a little time arranging the centerpiece, twisting the spirals together and over each other with your fingers to create a solid front. You can add more spirals if you want a fuller effect.

Vintage Choker

With its use of black beads and wire, this choker harks back to the very early years of the nineteenth century, when blackened, steel jewelry was very popular, particularly in Paris, and to the black jet jewelry of the Victorian era. It looks equally attractive worn with jeans or a classic black dress.

The number of beads depends on the look you want to create. If you are using small beads to make a delicate-looking choker, you will need up to 40 assorted black and silver beads; for a chunky frontpiece, 12–14 beads will be sufficient.

MATERIALS
- Approx. 14' (4.25m) 24-gauge (0.6mm) black iron wire
- Selection of black and silver beads in different shapes and sizes, ranging from 3–4mm to 8–10mm

TOOLS
- Round- and flat-nose pliers
- Wire cutters
- Mandrel or dowel
- Table vise
- Hand drill

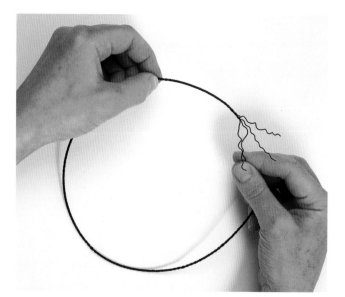

STEP 1 Cut four 20-in. (50-cm) lengths of 24-gauge (0.6mm) black iron wire. Bind the ends together with masking tape and straighten by pulling the wire through your fingers. Place one taped end in the table vise and the other in the chuck of the hand drill, and twist (see page 17). Remove from the drill and vise and cut off the taped ends. Unravel approximately 1½" (4cm) at one end of the twist and separate all the wires.

STEP 2 Wrap three of the four wires around the twisted stem a couple of times to secure. Snip off any spiky ends.

STEP 3 Using your round-nose pliers, curl the end of the remaining wire into a small loop. Create a second, much larger loop by curling the wire in the opposite direction, just under the first circle, to complete the fish-hook clasp. Hammer the end of the fish-hook clasp to flatten and work-harden it (see page 17).

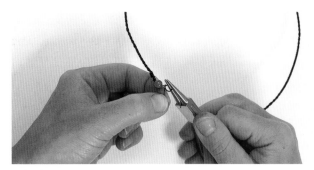

STEP 4 To form the eye of the clasp, unravel the wires on the opposite end of the twist, as in Step 2, and separate them out. Wrap three of the wires around the stem of the twist, until you are left with just one wire protruding. Thread a bead onto this wire, making sure that you still have at least 1" (2.5cm) left to create the eye. Bend this wire at right angles and then form a loop around your round-nose pliers, with the end overlapping the stem.

STEP 5 Secure the wire by wrapping it around the stem a couple of times. Cut off any excess. Hammer the end of the loop, as in Step 3, to work-harden it.

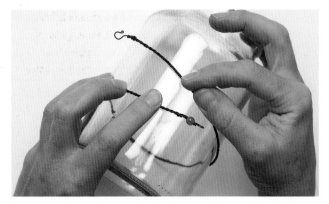

STEP 6 To create the circular shape of the choker, find a cylindrical object about 4" (10cm) in diameter (such as a bottle or cookie jar) and wrap the twisted wires around it tightly, overlapping the ends.

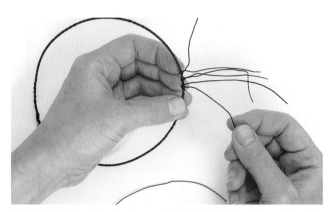

STEP 7 Cut at least eleven 7–9-in. (18–20-cm) lengths of 24-gauge (0.6mm) black iron wire. Find the center of the choker ring and wrap the center of the first wire around it, twisting it around several times to secure.

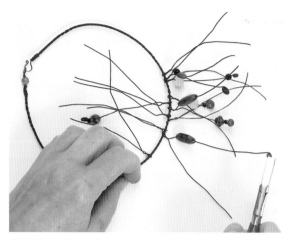

STEP 8 Continue until you have used up all the wires, making sure that they are centered on the front of the choker ring. Begin threading beads of varying shapes and sizes onto the ends of the wires.

STEP 9 Curl spirals at the ends of the wires (see page 16) to secure the beads. Work outward from the center to ensure the piece does not end up lopsided.

STEP 10 Spiral any loose ends of wire and wrap the wires over each other to link the elements together and form a solid framework.

VARIATION: Chunky Purple Choker

Experiment with different-colored wires and beads. The choker ring in this piece was made from two lengths of 20-gauge (0.8mm) silver wire twisted together, with a selection of chunky beads in purple tones threaded onto the extending wires.

Waterfall Chain Necklace

This is a great recycling project—a design that enables you to use up tiny lengths of broken silver chain, shimmering like sunlight shining on a waterfall. For a classic, symmetrical centerpiece, cut the chain into regular lengths or shape it to a tapered point. For a more contemporary fashion statement, make an asymmetric unit with different types of chain suspended at different levels.

MATERIALS
- Approx. 20" (50cm) ready-made silver trace chain
- 24 red size 8° seed beads
- 12" (30cm) 24- and 20-gauge (0.6mm and 0.8mm) silver wire

TOOLS
- Round- and flat-nose pliers
- Wire cutters

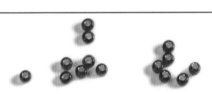

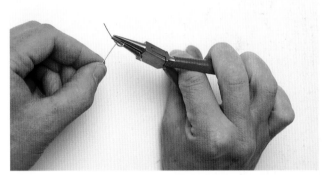

STEP 1 Cut a 2-in. (5-cm) length of 20-gauge (0.8mm) silver wire. Place your round-nose pliers in the center of the wire and twist the ends around in opposite directions, so that they cross over each other to form a loop.

STEP 2 Using your round-nose pliers, curl each end outward to form a small circle. You have now created the "hanger" for the waterfall chain.

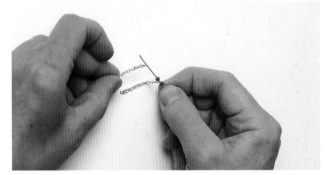

STEP 3 Cut a 1½-in. (4-cm) length of 20-gauge (0.8mm) wire and, using your round-nose pliers, make a link at one end (see page 14). Feed a red size 8° seed bead onto this wire and push it toward the link. Thread a small piece of ready-made chain onto the wire and push it toward the seed bead. Continue in this way, alternating chain and beads. The beads will keep the lengths of chain slightly separate from one another.

STEP 4 When you have used up eight seed beads and seven lengths of chain, curl the end of the wire into a link (see page 14).

STEP 5 Decide whether you want the chains to be the same length or to taper toward the center, and then cut to the desired length.

STEP 6 Using 24-gauge (0.6mm) wire, make seven jump rings (see page 16). Thread each jump ring with a single red seed bead.

STEP 7 Connect one beaded jump ring to the ends of each of the suspended chains and press closed with your flat-nose pliers.

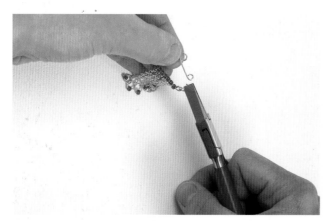

STEP 8 Make two more jump rings out of 20-gauge (0.8mm) wire and connect the hanger unit made in Step 1 to the suspended-chain unit.

STEP 9 Thread a seed bead onto a 1-in. (2.5-cm) piece of wire and make a link at one end and a head pin at the other (see page 15). Using your flat-nose pliers, connect the linked bead to the center of the hanger unit.

STEP 10 Take a ready-made chain and divide it into sections about 1½" (4cm) long by opening the links. Intersperse threaded beads (see page 14) between the sections. When the chain is the length you want it to be, connect the hanger to the center of the chain by using a jump ring.

VARIATION: # Asymmetric Necklace

For an asymmetric effect, use different types, colors, thicknesses, and lengths of chain. Suspend them from a wire threaded with small seed beads.

Beaded Cross

Threaded onto velvet or organza ribbon, these contemporary beaded crosses make a stunning fashion statement. For a wedding necklace, make the cross with pearls or crystals and suspend it from a choker of freshwater pearls or a simple gold chain. Alternatively, for a special birthday gift, make a cross from beads in the recipient's birthstone.

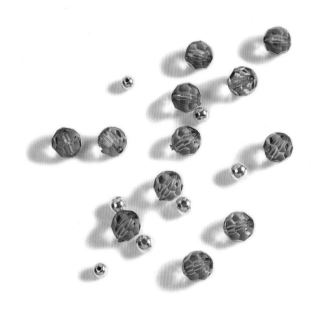

STEP 1 Cut a 9-in. (23-cm) length of 20-gauge (0.8mm) silver wire. Measure 4" (10cm) from one end of the wire and bend the wire around your round-nose pliers at this point to form a U-shape. Squeeze the wire around the circular shape with the tips of your flat- (or chain-) nose pliers to form a circular end.

<table>
<tr><td>

MATERIALS
- 8" (20cm) 24-gauge (0.6mm) silver wire
- 6 faceted 8mm amethyst beads
- 1 silver 4mm bead
- 1 clear 4–5mm clear bead
- Pink organza ribbon, ½" (1cm) wide
- Glue (optional)

TOOLS
- Round-, flat-, and chain-nose pliers
- Wire cutters
- Hammer and flat steel block

</td></tr>
</table>

STEP 2 Gently flatten and work-harden the end of the circle by tapping it on a steel block (see page 19). The two parallel wires will move apart and will need to be pushed back into position.

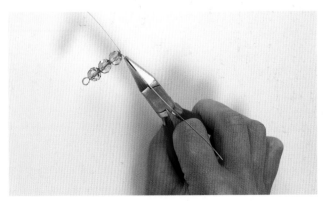

STEP 3 Thread three of the 8mm amethyst beads onto the doubled, parallel wires, sliding them up to the circular end. Using your flat-nose pliers, bend each wire outward at right angles.

STEP 4 From each of these bends, measure ½" (1cm) and, using the tip of your flat-nose pliers, fold the end of the wire back in the opposite direction to make the arms of the cross. Using your flat-nose pliers, squeeze the wires together so that there is no space between them.

STEP 5 Thread one 8mm amethyst bead onto each arm of the cross.

STEP 6 Press the beads in firmly toward the center of the cross and, using the tips of your round-nose pliers, partially loop the wire toward the back of the cross. Stop when it touches the bead. Squeeze the looped wires together with your flat-nose pliers to form a head pin to prevent the beads from slipping off.

STEP 7 Fold the wires up at right angles, near the bead holes, to complete the cross shape. Thread the last amethyst bead onto the vertical, doubled wires.

STEP 8 Wrap the shorter wire around the longer one, near the top of the bead hole, to secure. Snip off any excess wire and press with your flat-nose pliers to neaten.

STEP 9 Thread a 4mm silver bead onto the single wire, just above the wrapped wire. Using your round-nose pliers, form a link (see page 14). Secure by wrapping the wire around the stem a couple of times, then snip off any excess and neaten.

STEP 10 For added decoration, create a pendant drop with a 4–5mm clear bead and a wire spiral and attach it to the base of the cross.

STEP 11 Make two coils of wire about ½" (1cm) long (see page 16). Cut the wire off the spool, leaving about 1" (2.5cm) extending. Curl the extending wire around the tip of your round-nose pliers until it touches the coil.

STEP 12 Cut a piece of ribbon for the choker. Feed one end into a coil and, using your flat-nose pliers, squeeze the last rung of the coil to hold it firmly in place. If you wish, add a little glue for added security.

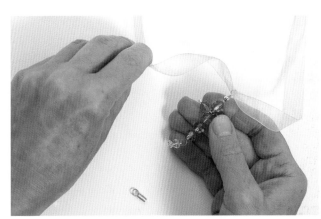

STEP 13 Thread the cross onto the ribbon. Attach the second coil in the same way. Make a clasp of your choice (see pages 17 and 18 for examples of clasps) and attach to the loops at the ends of the coils.

VARIATION: Gothic Cross Choker

Following the instructions above, make the cross entirely from black faceted beads and stitch it lightly onto a black velvet choker. To fasten the choker, stitch a piece of black Velcro to either side of the back of the ribbon.

CHAPTER FIVE

Seasonal Styles

Inspired by nature and its changing cycles, I have designed a range of jewelry to represent the moods and atmosphere of the four seasons. Spring, bursting with new growth, features fresh, light-colored beads. Summer conjures up memories of ocean vacations and days spent in the sun. Fall is represented by fiery russets and golds, reminiscent of falling leaves. Finally, winter, which is cool and icy, uses crystals and clear glass beads to simulate the sparkling frosts and ice crystals. You can, of course, change the colors in all of these projects to suit your personal tastes.

Springtime Spiral Necklace

With the coming of spring and the soft light of longer days, new leaves slowly start to unfurl from their buds. That's the feeling that I wanted to capture with this striking design, in which a light-green focal bead is enclosed in a cone-shaped "cage" of wire, extending out to new growth. The spiral cone can also look very effective suspended on a leather choker or hung on a key ring. To make matching earrings, make two "caged" beads following Steps 1 through 6 of the necklace and suspend them from ready-made ear wires.

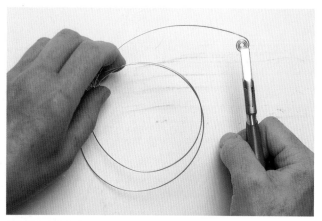

STEP 1 Working directly from a spool of 20-gauge (0.8mm) silver wire, curl the end of the wire into a small circle with the tips of your round-nose pliers. Hold the circle firmly in the jaws of your flat-nose pliers and spiral the wire around itself, until the spiral is approximately the same diameter as your largest bead. Cut the wire off the spool, leaving about 1" (2.5cm) to spare.

MATERIALS
- 20" (50cm) 20-gauge (0.8mm) silver wire
- 1 x 13mm green focal bead
- 1 x 8mm purple bead
- 1 x 6mm purple bead
- 26 purple size 6°seed beads
- 8" (20cm) ready-made chain

TOOLS
- Round- and flat-nose pliers
- Wire cutters
- Hammer and steel block

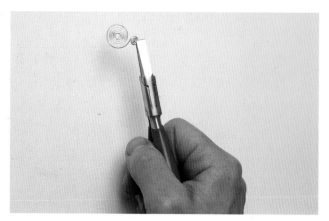

STEP 2 Curl this extended wire into a tiny spiral in the opposite direction to the first, until it meets the large spiral.

STEP 3 Hold the central loop of the large spiral with the tip of your round-nose pliers and pull it outward, separating each coil to create a tapered, cone shape.

STEP 4 With your flat-nose pliers, fold the small spiral down at right angles to align with the end of the spiraling

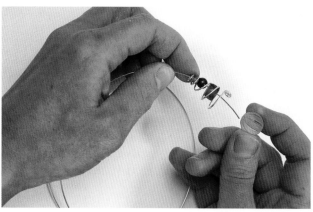

STEP 5 Working from the spool, thread 20-gauge (0.8mm) silver wire through the inside of the coned spiral, leaving about 1" (2.5cm) protruding at the wide end. Using beads in ascending size, thread the wire with beads, pushing them as far up the spiral as they will go to fill the space.

STEP 6 Cut the wire off the spool. Using your round-nose pliers, make a head pin (see page 15) against the last and largest bead hole, securing it at the end of the cone, and a link at the other end of the wire.

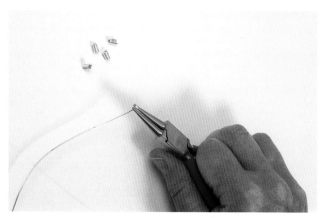

STEP 7 Using the tips of your round-nose pliers or a spiral bead maker, curl 12 little "springs" of coiled wire about ½" (1cm) long.

STEP 8 Thread 20-gauge (0.8mm) wire through these coils and plug each end with a size 6° seed bead. Snip off the excess wire and make a link (see page 14) at each end.

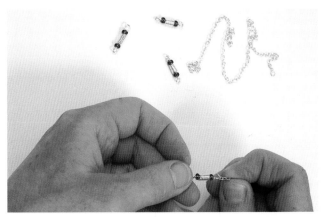

STEP 9 Cut the ready-made chain into ten ½-in. (1-cm) sections and two 1½-in. (3.5-cm) sections. Connect all the units together, alternating the beaded coils and the sections of chain, leaving the two longest sections of chain at the back of the necklace to connect to the fastener.

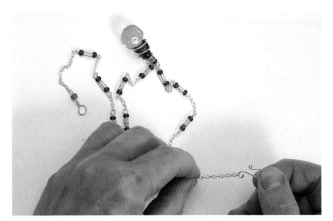

STEP 10 Open the link at the top of the spiral beaded cone and connect it to the center of the chain necklace. Finish by making an end clasp of your choice (see pages 17 and 18).

VARIATION: Single-color Inverted Spirals

Limiting the range of colors and inverting the spiral so that the widest end is at the top creates a very dramatic look. The necklace on the left was made using metallic beads, while the one on the right incorporates beads of jet-black and metallic silver.

Summer Seashell Necklace

With its pale, sun-bleached colors, this casual corded necklace has a lovely summery feel—the perfect way to show off a light tan! You can buy pre-drilled shells from bead suppliers. The necklace is fastened by attaching the fish-hook clasp to any point between the knots in the cord, so it can be adjusted to suit all shapes and sizes!

> ### MATERIALS
> - Approx. 60" (1.5m) natural-colored coated cotton cord
> - 30–40 assorted shells
> - Approx. 15 size 8° turquoise seed beads
> - 24-gauge (0.6mm) and 20-gauge (0.8mm) silver wire
> - Superglue (optional)
> ### TOOLS
> - Round- and flat-nose pliers
> - Wire cutters
> - Hammer and steel block (optional)

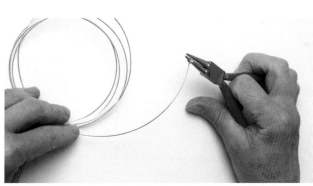

STEP 1 To make the eye for the fish-hook clasp, wrap 20-gauge (0.8mm) wire around the tip of your round-nose pliers ten to twelve times to make a tight, even coil about ¼" (6mm) long. The coil needs to be wide enough to slide onto doubled-up cord. Alternatively, you could wrap the wire around a knitting needle or a mandrel.

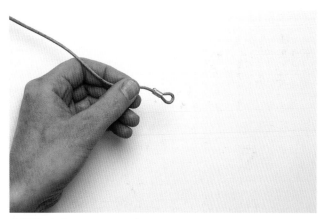

STEP 2 Cut a length of cord about three times as long as you want the finished necklace to be. Slide the wire coil onto the cord and then double the cord back on itself, feeding it back through the coil to form a loop.

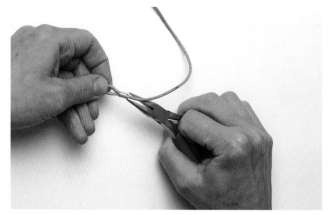

STEP 3 Using flat-nose pliers, squeeze the first and last loop of the coil tightly onto the cord to secure it firmly in place. If you wish, you can add a little superglue for extra strength and security.

STEP 4 Thread the shells with 24-gauge (0.6mm) wire, forming a head pin at one end and a link at the other (see page 15). For variety, thread several small shells onto one wire and add turquoise seed beads.

STEP 5 Make jump rings (see page 16) from 20-gauge (0.8mm) wire and loop them through the top links of the shells. Fasten the jump rings around the cord and close with flat-nose pliers, knotting the cord on each side to hold the shells in position. In places, group two or three shells together for added fullness.

STEP 6 Following the instructions in Step 1, make a coil of wire that is just wide enough to slip over the cord, leaving about 1" (2.5cm) protruding. With your round-nose pliers, curl a tiny loop at the end of the protruding wire.

STEP 7 Place the widest part of the round-nose pliers just under this first loop, and curl it in the opposite direction to form a fish-hook clasp.

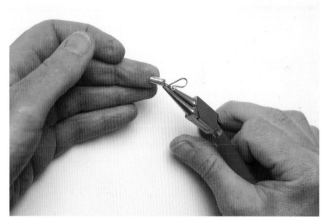

STEP 8 Bend the fish-hook clasp so that it sits vertically above the coil. (You can toughen this hook by gently hammering it on a steel block—see page 19.)

STEP 9 Slide the fish-hook clasp onto the end of the cord and secure it by squeezing the last loop of the coil with your flat-nose pliers.

STEP 10 Using jump rings, connect and suspend a bunch of linked shells from the end of the loop.

VARIATION: Colored Glass Beads

Cord comes in many different colors. Thread beads onto colored wires to coordinate with whatever color of cord you are using.

Falling Leaves Necklace

Beaded leaves in autumnal shades of copper and bronze form the centerpiece of this stylish necklace. If this particular design is too elaborate for your tastes, simplify it by using just three leaf units on a ready-made chain. The wire leaves can be attached to many other things, too. Why not use them as decorations for greetings cards and scrapbook layouts or as gift tags?

MATERIALS
- Approx. 75 size 11° gold-colored seed beads
- Six 6mm copper-colored beads
- One oblong focal bead, about 20mm long
- Eight 8mm brown and two 10mm light-brown faceted beads
- 20- and 26-gauge (0.8mm and 0.4mm) copper wire

TOOLS
- Round- and flat-nose pliers
- Wire cutters
- Hammer and steel block

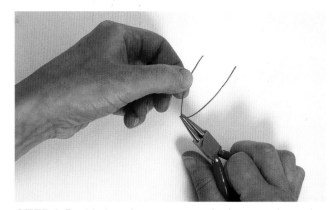

STEP 1 Decide how long you want the leaves to be and cut just over double that amount of 20-gauge (0.8mm) copper wire for each one. For example, to make a leaf 1½" (4cm) long, you will need about 4" (10cm) of wire. Bend the wire in two, just past the halfway point, so that one section is slightly longer than the other.

VARIATION: Leaf Earrings

Follow Steps 1 through 8 to make two identical leaves. Make two jump rings and suspend the leaves from ready-made ear wires.

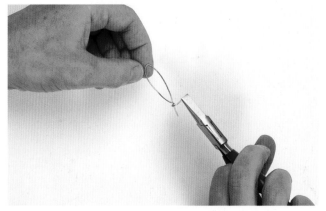

STEP 2 Using your flat-nose pliers, wrap the longer end of wire tightly around the shorter wire two or three times and snip off any excess, leaving the shorter wire extending by about ½" (1cm).

STEP 3 At the other end of the leaf, squeeze the wires together with your flat-nose pliers, leaving a narrow channel between them.

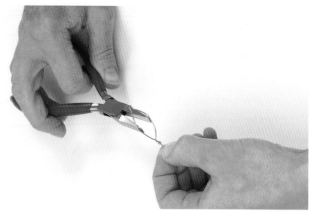

STEP 4 Place your flat-nose pliers in the space between the wires at the center of the leaf and gently pry the wires apart by opening the pliers. Using your flat-nose pliers, spend a little time adjusting the piece into a leaf shape.

STEP 5 Hammer the wire frame on your steel block to work-harden it, avoiding the wrapped end (see page 19).

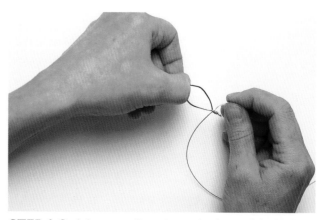

STEP 6 Curl the extending wire at the base of the leaf into a link with your round-nose pliers (see page 14). Wrap 26-gauge (0.4mm) wire around the top of the leaf (just under the link).

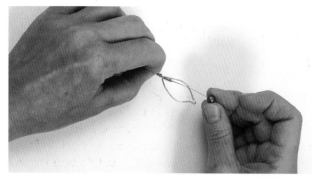

STEP 7 Pull this narrow wire straight down the center of the leaf shape and cut it off from the spool, leaving at least ½" (1cm) extending beyond the end of the leaf. Thread gold seed beads onto this wire all the way up to the tip of the leaf, with one 6mm copper bead in the center as a focal bead.

STEP 8 Using your flat-nose pliers, wrap any excess wire around the end tip of the leaf a couple of times to secure it.

STEP 9 Make three more leaves in the same way. Then make two small leaves, using about 2½" (7cm) of 20-gauge wire and thread them with 6–8 seed beads. Finally, make a large leaf from 6" (15cm) of wire, and thread it with the oblong focal bead at the center, with one 6mm copper bead and two seed beads on either side of it, as shown.

STEP 10 Make a beaded chain by threading four 8mm faceted brown beads, linked together with jump rings, followed by two 10mm lighter brown beads and four more 8mm beads.

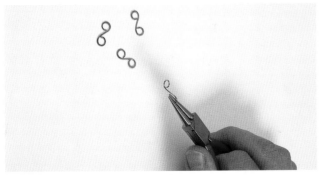

STEP 11 Cut twelve 1-in. (2.5-cm) pieces of 20-gauge (0.8mm) copper wire. Curl half of each piece around your round-nose pliers, then turn the wire over, and curl the remainder in the opposite direction to make an S-shape.

STEP 12 Connect the S-shapes together with jump rings (see page 16) to make two chains of six S-shapes each, and attach one to each side of the beaded chain made in Step 10. Suspend the largest leaf from the jump ring between the largest two beads of the beaded chain, with two medium leaves and one small leaf on either side of it. Create a clasp for the necklace (see pages 17 and 18).

VARIATION: Corey Corded Leaf Choker

For a simple, more casual design, make one large leaf and suspend it from a cord. To make the fastener at the end of the choker, make two coils of wire that fit the diameter of the cord. Cut the coil off the wire spool, leaving 1" (2.5cm) of wire extending, and curl the ends into links. Slide the coils onto the ends of the cord and secure by squeezing the last rung of the coil tightly against the cord with your flat-nose pliers. (You can apply a little adhesive for added security!) Attach a fish-hook clasp (see page 17) to the links at the ends of the coils.

Winter Frost Necklace

Winter frost and ice were the inspiration for this necklace, which is made up of clear glass beads amd crystals. As it is so neutral in coloring, it can be worn with any outfit and will suit both young and old. However, if you want a more colorful feel, simply use different tones and hues. Matching earrings can be created using a variety of threaded beads and "feathers" suspended from ear wires.

I used a ready-made chain, although you could, of course, make your own. Whichever you choose, check that the links are large enough to take the 20-gauge (0.8mm) wire used to thread the beads.

STEP 1 Thread your beads with wire, forming a head pin at one end and a link at the other (see page 15).

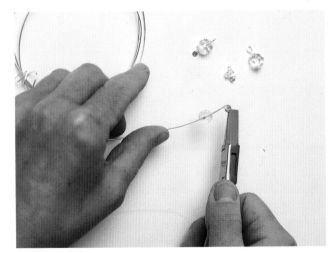

STEP 2 As an alternative to a head pin, you could spiral the end of the wire (see page 16).

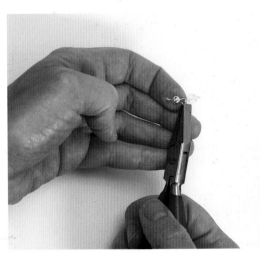

STEP 3 If you are using very small beads, link some together in a chainlike formation.

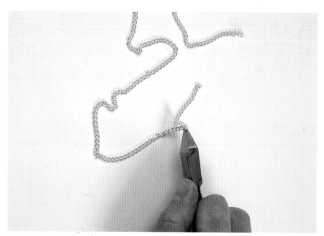

STEP 4 Cut a 17-in. (42.5-cm) length of ready-made chain and snip 2" (5cm) off the end.

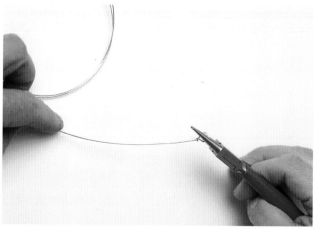

STEP 5 Curl a length of wire around your round-nose pliers to make a loop, and wrap the excess around itself, as you would when making the eye of a clasp. Leave a length of wire stem free so that you can add on a bead. (The length depends on the size of the bead you have chosen.)

STEP 6 Thread a clear bead onto the end of this wire and curl the other end into a link (see page 14).

STEP 7 Attach the link to one end of the 2-in. (5-cm) piece of chain and close with flat-nose pliers to secure.

STEP 8 Make jump rings (see page 16) and connect your threaded beads to the large loop in the 2-in. (5-cm) chain, starting with smaller beads at one end, increasing in size as you near the center, and finishing with smaller beads at the other end of the chain.

STEP 9 Cut 4–6 pieces of wire 1–1½" (2.5–4cm) in length. Curl one end into a link with your round-nose pliers (see page 14), threading with beads if desired. Gently hammer the other end on a steel block until the wire spreads into a "feather" shape.

STEP 10 Link these wire "feathers" in between the beads to add sparkle to your icy cascade. (Alternatively, you could connect fine pieces of silver chain among the beads.)

STEP 11 Thread the cascade of beads onto the 15-in. (37.5-cm) length of chain and connect a clasp to the ends.

VARIATION: # Green Bead Cascade

These bead bunches, or cascades, can be made from any range of assorted beads. In fact, it's a great way of using up odd beads from old, broken necklaces, giving them a new lease on life! This green cascade has silver "hieroglyphs" between the beads (created in the same way as in the Hieroglyphic Charm Necklace on page 96) for added decoration.

CHAPTER SIX

Charm Designs

Always fashionable and fun, the appeal of charm jewelry lies in bringing together an eclectic combination of items to make a piece that is very personal to the wearer. You might, for example, choose to incorporate coins, shells, and stones that you have picked up on your travels. Perhaps you prefer to create your own charms, in the form of glyphs and symbols (real or invented), or to create beaded strands of color. You can even combine all these ideas, and more, in the same design! The projects in this chapter give you the opportunity to make a very individual style statement, in which you can let your imagination run wild!

Hieroglyphic Charm Necklace

The wire "hieroglyphs" on this necklace are ones that I devised myself,
but you can use any wiggly wire pattern of your own creation.
Experiment and develop your own wire shapes, so that
your charm necklace is completely unique!

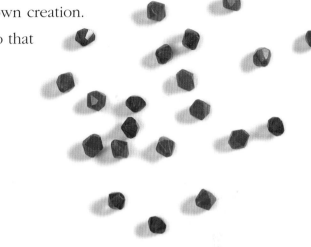

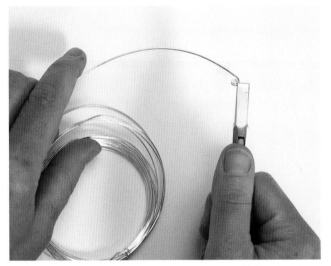

STEP 1 Working from a spool of 20-gauge (0.8mm) wire,
make a little hook at the end of the wire using your round-
nose pliers. Coil this wire around itself in a spiral, holding it
steady with your flat-nose pliers.

MATERIALS
- 30" (75cm) 20-gauge (0.8mm) silver wire
- 16" (40cm) ready-made chain
- 10 x 4mm red beads

TOOLS
- Round- and flat-nose pliers
- Wire cutters
- Hammer and steel stake

STEP 2 Bend the wire around the tip of your round-nose
pliers to create a wiggly shape.

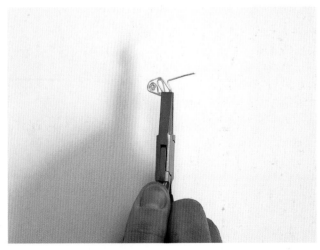

STEP 3 Bend the wire around the outline of the wiggly
shape to frame it. Cut the wire off the spool, leaving enough
to thread on a bead plus about ½" (1cm). Bend the
extending wire at 90°.

STEP 4 Feed a 4mm red bead onto the extending wire and push it up to the bend in the wire.

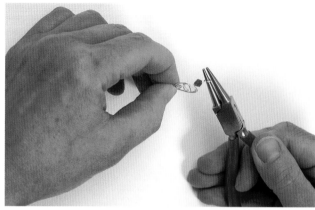

STEP 5 Using your round-nose pliers, make a link at the end of the extending wire (see page 14).

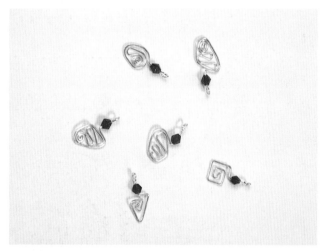

STEP 6 Make nine more "hieroglyphs" in the same way. The hieroglyphs can be different shapes and styles, but try to keep them roughly the same size.

STEP 7 Gently hammer the ends of the hieroglyphs on a steel block, making sure you avoid the beads, to work-harden and spread the wire. Alternatively, flatten the units in the jaws of your flat-nose pliers.

STEP 8 Find the center of your ready-made chain. Undo the link at the top of one of the hieroglyphs and attach it to the central link of the chain, closing up the link again with your flat-nose pliers. If the 20-gauge (0.8mm) wire does not fit into the chain, make small jump rings from finer wire.

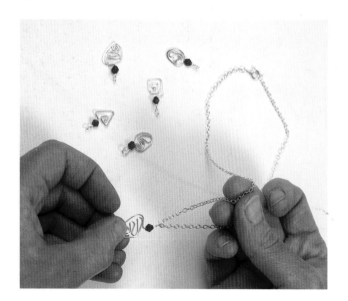

STEP 9 Continue to connect the units on either side of the central link of the necklace, leaving about six chain links in between each one, until you have suspended nine units from the front of the chain.

STEP 10 So that the necklace can be worn at varying lengths, make seven jump rings (see page 16) and link them together to form a chain about 1" (2.5cm) long. Attach this chain to the back "eye" clasp of the necklace and suspend the last remaining hieroglyph from it to create an attractive decorative finish.

VARIATION:

Colored Hieroglyph Necklace

For a more casual and informal-looking piece, make the wire hieroglyphs from brightly colored wires. When flattening the units, be careful not to hammer too hard, as you could chip off the outer color enamel coating of the wire. To make matching earrings, follow Steps 1 through 5 of the necklace. Make two wire spirals and glue a flat post earring finding to the back of each one. Connect the hieroglyph to the wire spirals and suspend it from the bottom loop.

Belly Dancer's Bracelet

Dangling silver and gold coin decorations give this bracelet an exotic flavor!
To make matching earrings, connect three of the looped silver units together
with jump rings to form an inverted triangle, attach a pair of coin decorations to the lowest
loop, and suspend the entire piece from ready-made earwires. You could also extend the
bracelet into a necklace by attaching a piece of ready-made chain to each side.

MATERIALS
- Approx. 3' (1m) 20-gauge wire (0.8mm) silver wire
- 18 gold- and 18 silver-colored metal "coin-like" decorations about ½" (1.5cm) in diameter

TOOLS
- Round- and flat-nose pliers
- Wire cutters
- Hammer and steel block

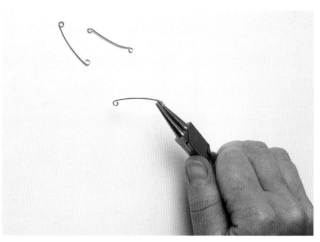

STEP 1 Cut eighteen 1½-in. (4-cm) lengths of 20-gauge (0.8mm) silver wire. Using the tips of your round-nose pliers, curl the ends into small loops, curling them in toward each other.

STEP 2 Find the center of the looped wire and mold it around the widest part of your round-nosed pliers, making sure that the loops curl outward on each side. Flatten and work-harden each unit by gently hammering it on a steel block (see page 19).

STEP 3 Make jump rings (see page 16) and connect the coins together in pairs, with one gold and one silver coin in each pair.

STEP 4 Connect the looped units into a chain, using jump rings.

STEP 5 Attach one pair of coins to each looped unit, closing the jump rings with your flat-nose pliers. Make a fish-hook clasp (see page 17) to close the bracelet.

Cascade Ring

This is primarily a "party" ring, something for the girl who has everything! The cascade, or bead bunch, at the front can be as full as you wish. For a very full cascade, use up to 20 beads. Made from gold or silver wire and decorated with pearls, it can look very dressy and elegant. For a more up-to-the-minute, trendy look, use colored wires and beads that provide a striking color contrast.

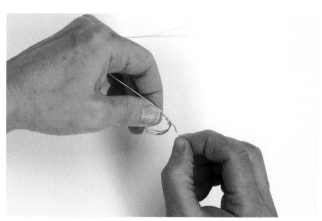

MATERIALS
- Approx. 3' (1m) 20-gauge (0.8mm) silver wire
- Selection of 2mm–8mm beads

TOOLS
- Ring mandrel or dowel
- Hammer
- Round- and flat-nose pliers
- Wire cutters

STEP 1 Wrap 20-gauge (0.8mm) silver wire three or four times around a ring mandrel that is one size smaller than the ring size you require, making one of the wraps looser than the others so that you create a small gap. If you do not have a ring mandrel, use a piece of dowel slightly smaller than you want the ring to be.

STEP 2 Slide the wrapped coils off the mandrel, holding them firmly with your fingers to maintain the circular shape. Secure the coils by wrapping the cut end of wire around the circular ring shank.

STEP 3 Cut the wire off the spool, leaving 4–6" (10–15cm) extending. Wrap this wire around the wire coils, spacing the wraps apart to create interestingly shaped curves on the surface and making sure that one of the wraps is made loose, so that there is a gap where the cascade of beads will be attached. Secure the end of the wire by binding it around the shank of the ring.

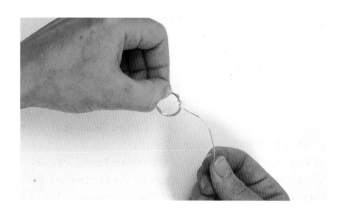

STEP 4 Place the bound ring back on the mandrel and gently hammer it all the way around, flattening and spreading the wire. Take the ring off the mandrel, turn it upside down, and replace it, then hammer again. This step is to ensure that the wire is flattened evenly and that you do not end up with one edge fatter than the other.

STEP 5 Thread your chosen beads onto wire, making a head pin at one end and a link at the other (see pages 14–15). Spiral some of the head pins for a decorative finish (see page 16) and leave others plain.

STEP 6 Make jump rings (see page 16) to suspend the threaded beads. For a fuller, bunched effect, you can link two or three of the smaller threaded beads together on one jump ring.

STEP 7 Link all the threaded beads in a chain to produce a cascade, or bunch. Keep adding threaded beads until you are satisfied! Use a jump ring to attach the cascade to the front of the ring, through the gap that you created in Step 1.

Bead Charm Necklace

If you're new to making wire jewelry, this is a great piece to start with as it gives you the chance to practice many different ways of threading beads and connecting different elements together. Before you begin, spend time looking at the colors and shapes of your beads and other decorations to ensure that they work well together. I put in lots of charms, because I like the richness of having them packed closely together, but a few randomly scattered beads can look just as effective.

MATERIALS
- Selection of beads in different shapes and sizes, ranging from 4 to 12mm
- 4–6 coin findings
- Approx. 6' (2m) 20-gauge (0.8mm) gold wire
- Approx. 16" (40cm) ready-made chain

TOOLS
- Round- and flat-nose pliers
- Wire cutters
- Hammer and steel block

STEP 1 First, make up the individual charms. One option is to thread your beads onto wires, forming links at one end and head pins or spirals at the other (see pages 14–16).

STEP 2 If you have lots of tiny beads, you can link two or more together in short chains.

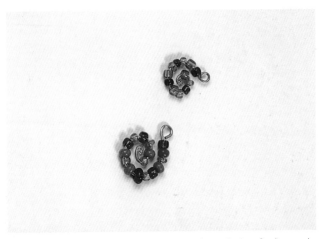

STEP 3 For added color, you can make spirals of wire and thread them with seed beads.

STEP 4 To make wire "feathers," cut 1-in. (2-5-cm) lengths of wire. Form a link at one end (see page 14), and hammer the other end on a steel block, so that it flattens and spreads into a feather shape.

STEP 5 You can also form curly wiggles of wire, as in the Hieroglyphic Charm Necklace on page 96.

STEP 6 Select a ready-made chain that can be threaded with 20-gauge (0.8mm) jump rings, cut a 7-in. (18-cm) length, and make a beaded link to attach to each end (see page 14). This will be the "charm" part of the necklace. Work out the order that you want the charms to go in.

VARIATION: Bead Charm Bracelet and Earrings

Create a bracelet in the same way as the necklace, adding a clasp at the end of Step 7 and omitting Step 8. For bold, matching earrings, make two bead bunches (as in the Cascade Ring on page 102), and attach them to ready-made ear wires.

STEP 7 Make jump rings (see page 16) and attach the charms to the chain.

STEP 8 Connect enough ready-made chain on each side of the charm chain to extend the necklace to the length you want. Make a clasp (see pages 17–18) and attach to each end of the necklace.

VARIATION: Bold Decorative Necklaces

For a more opulent-looking version, use a rich jade and gold color scheme and intersperse caged glass beads (made following the instructions for the Springtime Spiral Necklace on page 78) with gold spirals and twists. Alternatively, gold-colored coins (such as the ones used in the Belly Dancer's Bracelet on page 100), semiprecious chip beads, and gold-wire hieroglyphic symbols (as created in the Hieroglyphic Charm Necklace on page 96), make a striking decoration.

CHAPTER SEVEN

Classic Jewelry

I've always been fascinated by ancient cultures and the artifacts that they produced. In this chapter I've tried to capture the essence of some of my favorite traditional crafts from around the world, ranging from the tribal masks and carvings that I first saw as a child growing up in East and West Africa to the wonderful gold jewelry of the Aztecs. Have fun exploring!

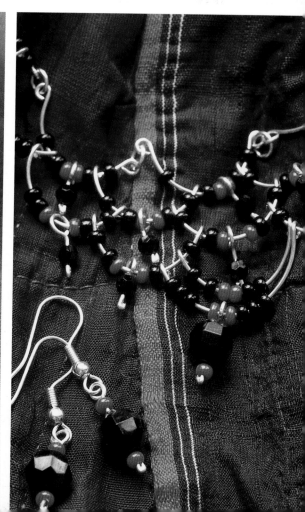

Indian Spice Necklace

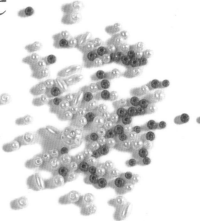

This necklace was inspired by the delicate filigree work that is characteristic of traditional Indian jewelry—in particular, the ornate forehead decorations that are created for Indian brides. The colors chosen are reminiscent of the warm glow of tasty, exotic spices. The overall effect is very ornate and intricate —guaranteed to impress!

MATERIALS
- Approx. 5' (1.6m) 20-gauge (0.8mm) gold wire
- Orange-colored and pearl 3mm seed beads
- Fifteen 4mm pearl beads
- 18mm pearl focal bead
- Approx. 6" (15cm) ready-made trace chain

TOOLS
- Round- and flat-nose pliers
- Wire cutters
- Dowel about ½" (12mm) in diameter

STEP 1 Working from the spool, coil the wire around the dowel 16 to 17 times.

STEP 2 Cut each circle off the coil, just as you would to make jump rings (see page 16). Using your wire cutters, snip about ½" (1cm) out of one of the circles. Discard the snipped-out piece. Place the remainder against each full circle in turn and use it as a guide to remove the same amount of wire. You should now have 15 scalloped shapes.

STEP 3 Using the ends of your round-nose pliers, curl one end of five of these scallops into a link (see page 14). Thread two pearl, two orange, and two more pearl seed beads onto each curved scalloped piece and form a link at the other end of the wire.

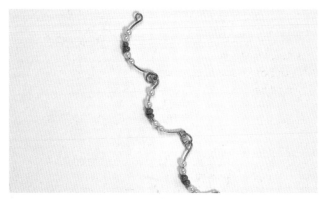

STEP 4 Make jump rings and link the five beaded scallops together to form the first row of the necklace, by connecting jump rings between the side loops.

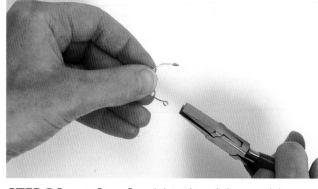

STEP 5 Repeat Steps 3 and 4 to thread the remaining ten scallops with seed beads. Using your flat-nose pliers, twist the links at each side 90° so that they are at right angles to the row of beads.

STEP 6 Link four scallops directly onto the first row of the necklace by undoing the links. Position the first one between the last two pearl seed beads of the first scallop and the first two pearl seed beads of the second scallop on the top row, and continue until the row is complete.

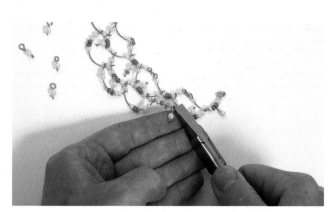

STEP 7 Continue adding rows of beaded scallops, using one less scallop in each row so that you end up with an inverted triangle.

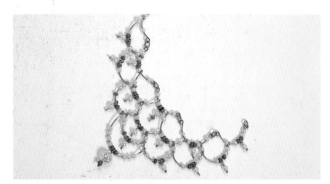

STEP 8 For added decoration, suspend a threaded pearl bead from the center of each scallop. Emphasize the final central scallop by repeating Steps 2 and 3 to make a larger scalloped wire to suspend either side of the last row, threading it with eight pearl seed beads and two orange ones, as shown, and suspend a large focal bead between the two orange seed beads.

STEP 9 Cut the ready-made chain into 1-in. (2.5-cm) sections. Thread small lengths of wire with one pearl, one orange, and one pearl seed bead. Connect the piece onto a ready-made chain interspersed with threaded beads.

VARIATION: Bold Color Contrasts

Strong color contrasts give the piece a very different look. Here, I substituted black and red beads for the orange and pearl seed beads and suspended a faceted black bead from the large scallop at the base. The result is much bolder in appearance and could be worn with casual clothes, whereas the "Indian" version is more formal and "dressy."

Far Eastern Promise

With its simple curves, reminiscent of temple roofs and Chinese and Japanese calligraphy, this necklace has a distinct flavor of the Orient. The hammering technique does take practice—but, as they say, practice makes perfect! If you find you've made a real mess of it, shape the ends of the hammered wires into little curls; the result will not look so Oriental, but it still will be very striking!

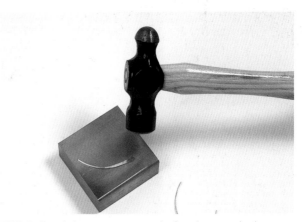

> ### MATERIALS
> - 30" (75cm) 18-gauge (1mm) silver wire
> ### TOOLS
> - Round- and flat-nose pliers
> - Wire cutters
> - Hammer and flat steel block
> - Dowels 1¼" (3cm) and ¾" (2cm) in diameter

STEP 1 For the centerpiece of your necklace, cut four 1½-in. (4-cm) lengths of wire and one 1-in. (2.5-cm) length. Shape the large pieces around the side of the larger dowel and the small piece around the smaller dowel.

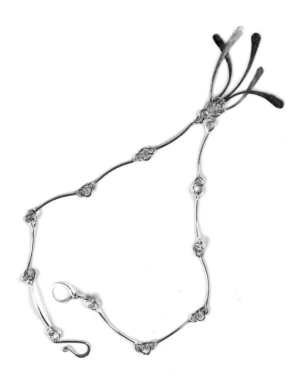

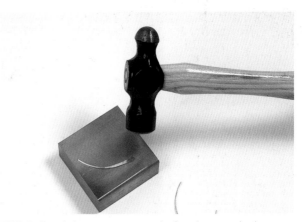

STEP 2 Gently hammer one end of each curved wire on a steel block until it spreads to a bulbous, paddle-shaped tip. Hammer both sides.

VARIATION: Hammered Wire Combinations

Experiment with curving and hammering wire to create different shape combinations. You can make more elaborate chains by linking two pieces together as one unit (and in varied metals).

STEP 3 Using your round-nose pliers, curl the unhammered ends into links, making sure that the links on two sets of the longer curves curl one way and two the other. The link on the short piece of wire can curve in whichever direction you choose.

STEP 4 Make a large jump ring (see page 16) and suspend the curved pieces from it, in the order shown. (The first piece should curve outward, the second inward, and the small piece in whichever direction you choose; the last two pieces should mirror the first.)

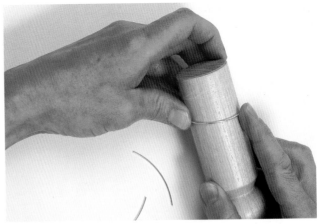

STEP 5 Work out how long you want the chain to be. Cut enough 2-in. (5-cm) lengths of 18-gauge (1mm) wire to make up this length (you will need an odd number of chain units). Curve the pieces around the large dowel.

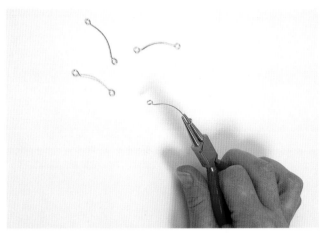

STEP 6 Using your round-nose pliers, form a link at each end of each curved piece (see page 14).

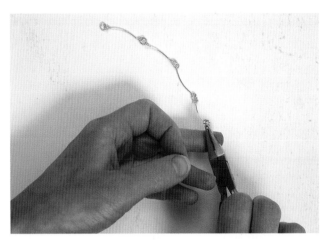

STEP 7 Make jump rings (see page 16) and join the curved units together to form a continuous chain.

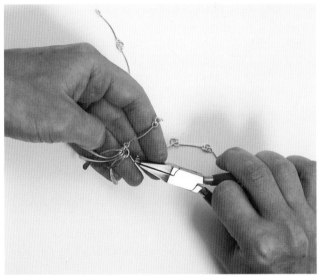

STEP 8 Attach the centerpiece to the central jump ring of the chain. Make a clasp (see page 17) and attach it to the ends of the chain.

VARIATION: Earrings

To make matching earrings, follow Steps 1 through 3 and make two 1-in. (2.5-cm) units. Suspend half the curved units on one jump ring and ear wire and half on another.

African Dream

Having spent my early childhood in Africa, I have always been inspired and influenced by African tribal art. Collared necklaces are traditionally worn to indicate status and wealth. Even though colored beads are often used, I decided to use wood and bone beads in my design as they remind me of all the wonderful traditional carvings that I have seen. The copper wire of the collar is intended to mimic the dusty red earth of the African plains.

If you have problems finding the cylindrical, carved beads, make the necklace out of suspended coils of wire (like narrow jump ring spirals) or suspend "stacks" of threaded beads from the collar.

MATERIALS
- 17 x 20mm cylindrical bone-effect beads
- 18 x 10mm square wooden beads
- 36" (90cm) 20-gauge (0.8mm) copper wire

TOOLS
- Round- and flat-nose pliers
- Wire cutters

STEP 1 Thread the cylindrical beads with 20-gauge (0.8mm) copper wire, forming a link at each end with your round-nose pliers (see page 14).

STEP 2 Do the same with the 18 wooden beads, so that each bead has a link at each end.

STEP 3 Make 17 jump rings (see page 16) and connect the wooden beads together to form the outline of your collar necklace.

STEP 4 Undo one link on each cylindrical bead and suspend the beads from the jump rings on the collar.

STEP 5 Working from the spool of wire, form a tiny hook with your round-nose pliers. Squash the hook with your flat-nose pliers and curl the wire around itself to form a small spiral (see page 16). Cut the wire off the spool, leaving just enough to form a small link at the end (see page 14). Make 17 spirals in this way.

VARIATION: Earrings

To make matching earrings, link a cylindrical bead and a wooden bead together, with a copper spiral at the base of the wooden bead, and suspend from ready-made ear wires.

STEP 6 Connect the spirals to the links at the end of the cylindrical bone beads.

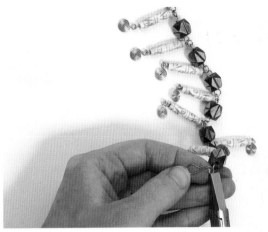

STEP 7 Make a fish-hook eye and clasp (see page 17) and attach to the ends of the necklace.

VARIATION: Black-Bead Necklace

This dramatic collared necklace was made from black wooden carved beads and threaded with black iron wire.

Aztec Tree of Life Necklace

The ancient Aztec civilization inspired me to create this turquoise and gold necklace. The Aztecs were renowned for the production of vivid precious-stone mosaics, and excelled in both stone and metal work. These designs were created as tributes to the gods, with the "tree" representing the cycle of life and the use of gold symbolizing the sun. Turquoise was worn by Aztec kings and is probably one of the oldest gemstones known. It was a sacred stone to the Aztecs as it was (and is still) attributed with healing powers.

Semiprecious chip stones can be purchased from bead or jewelry suppliers in 16- or 18-in. (40- or 45-cm) lengths. You may be surprised to discover just how inexpensive they can be!

MATERIALS
- 14" (35cm) 20-gauge (0.8mm) gold wire
- 12" (30cm) 26-gauge (0.4mm) gold wire
- 10–12 semiprecious turquoise drilled chip stones
- 2 x 4mm gold beads
- Ready-made wire choker

TOOLS
- Round- and flat-nose pliers
- Wire cutters
- Hammer and steel block

STEP 1 Cut approximately 14" (35cm) of 20-gauge (0.8mm) gold wire. Place your round-nose pliers in the center and bend the wire around them to form a circular shape. This is the base of the "tree."

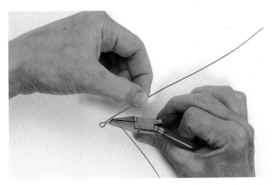

STEP 2 Straighten the extending wires so that they run parallel to each other. Hold one wire in your flat-nose pliers and bend it outward at right angles, just a little way up from the circular tip.

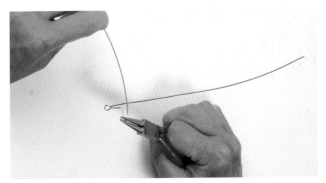

STEP 3 Between ¼ and ½" (0.5 and 1cm) from the bend, fold this wire back toward the other wire, bending it around your pliers to create a curved end. This is the first "branch" of the tree. The measurements do not have to be precise: the design is asymmetrical, so just follow your instincts as the pattern evolves.

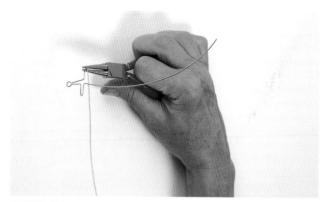

STEP 4 Straighten the wires so that they run parallel to each other again. Using your flat-nose pliers, repeat Steps 2 and 3 with the other wire to form another "branch" in the same way.

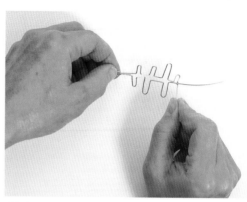

STEP 5 Make three or four branches on each side, starting with shorter branches about ¼–½" (0.5–1cm) long at the base, increasing to almost 1" (2.5cm) in the center, and reducing to ¼–½" (0.5–1cm) again at the top of the tree. When you reach the tip, secure the wires by wrapping one around the other two or three times.

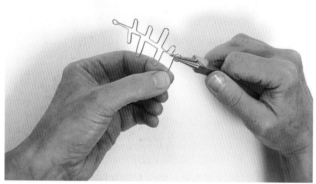

STEP 6 Form a link (see page 14) by curling the wire around your round-nose pliers. Secure the extending wire by wrapping it around itself. Press firmly with your flat-nose pliers and cut off any excess.

STEP 7 Hammer the tree very gently on a steel block to flatten and work-harden it, making sure you do not hammer the wrapped wire end.

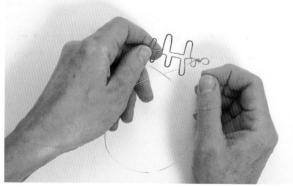

STEP 8 Snip off about 2" (5cm) of 26-gauge (0.4mm) wire and wrap it neatly around the top branch of the tree.

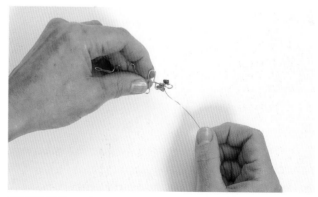

STEP 9 Thread a turquoise chip stone bead onto this wire and wrap the wire onto the wire branch below. Press with your flat-nose pliers to fix it firmly in place and cut off the excess wire.

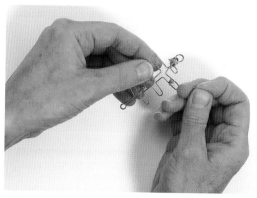

STEP 10 Continue threading stones onto the branches, wrapping the wire around as described in Step 9.

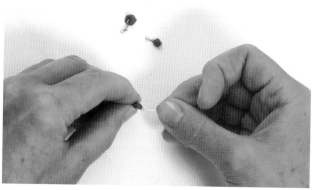

STEP 11 Create pendant drops by threading 26-gauge (0.8mm) wire through chip stone beads and wrapping one end around the other to secure. Form a link (see page 14) and cut off any excess wire.

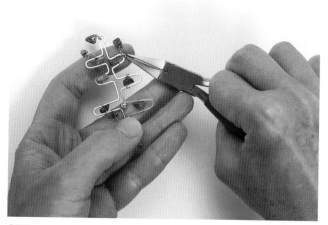

STEP 12 Make jump rings (see page 16) and attach the pendant drops to the ends of some of the branches.

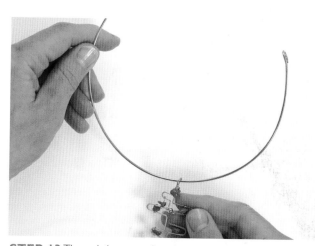

STEP 13 Thread the completed tree onto a ready-made choker.

VARIATION: Twisted Choker Ring

Make your own choker ring by twisting two or more wires together (see page 17). For a really individual gift, substitute the recipient's birthstone for the turquoise chips.

Glossary

Block A perfectly flat, polished block of steel, used with a flat-ended hammer to work-harden and temper metal.

Chip Irregular, semiprecious stone fragment that has been drilled and polished.

Crystal Natural, clear quartz gemstone.

Dowel A cylindrical object around which wire is curved. You could use a wooden dowel, a knitting needle, a rolling pin, the handle of a wooden spoon, a cookie jar, or anything cylindrical of the appropriate size.

Ear wires Earring hooks used to suspend beads or dangling drops to create earrings. Can be purchased ready made from jewelry and craft suppliers.

Findings A term used for jewelry components such as pin backs, chains, key rings, earring hooks and posts, and clasps.

Fish hook Wire clasp in the shape of a hook.

Gauge Refers to the thickness of wire. The smaller the number, the thicker the wire: for example, 14-gauge (1.5mm) wire, 18-gauge (1mm) wire, 20-gauge (0.8mm) wire, 24-gauge (0.6mm) wire, and 28-gauge (0.4mm) wire.

Head pin A wire that has been folded into a knob at the end to prevent beads from slipping off.

Jump ring Small, circular ring, used to link units together.

Link or Loop A full circle of wire, used for connecting or linking purposes.

Mandrel A circular rod, usually made from wood or steel, around which metal is curved.

Pliers Essential tool for gripping and bending wire.
   Chain-nose pliers
Pliers with smooth, tapering jaws used for intricate jewelry work. Sometimes referred to as snipe- or needle-nose pliers.
   Flat-nose pliers
Smooth-jawed, parallel pliers which provide a vise-like grip for holding wire.
   Round-nose pliers
Pliers with tapered, smooth conical jaws for curving wire and creating small loops.

S Link S-shaped wire link for connecting beads together to form a chain.

Seed bead Very small, round glass bead.

Shank The part of a ring that encircles the finger.

Spacer Bead or wire coil used between beads to separate and keep them apart.

Spool A coil of wire that can be obtained in measured reels from craft and hobby suppliers.

Stroke hammering A technique of gently hammering metal wire on a steel block to work-harden and flatten it without creating any texture on its surface.

Tempering To toughen or work-harden wire by hammering, coiling, twisting, or forming it, reducing its workability.

Wire cutters For wire work, small cutters with jaws that end in a point, allowing you to cut into small portions of wire from any angle. Sometimes referred to as snips.

Work-hardening Similar to tempering. Refers to the fact that the more you manipulate metal wire, the harder and less flexible it becomes. Gentle hammering helps to work-harden wire so that it becomes tough enough to withstand wear and tear without falling apart.

Suppliers

The beads and supplies used in this book are widely available through local and online bead shops, bead shows, and mail order catalogs. Some of the supplies used are from well-known brands. The contact information is listed even though some of these companies do not sell directly to the public.

US SUPPLIERS
Borosilicate glass beads:
Nancy Tobey Glass Beads
76 Pleasant St.
Ayer, MA 01432
(978) 772-3317
www.nancytobey.com

Buttons:
JHB International*
(303) 751-8100
www.buttons.com

Cast pewter beads:
Green Girl Studios
49 Reynolda Dr.
Asheville, NC 28803
(828) 298-2263
www.greengirlstudios.com

Dichroic glass beads and components:
Paula Radke Dichroic Glass Beads*
(800) 341-4945
www.paularadke.com

Etched shell pendants and beads:
Lillypilly Designs
PO Box 270136
Louisville, CO 80027
(303) 543-8673
www.lillypillydesigns.com

Hand-painted silk beads:
Kristal Wick Creations
6110 Dudley St.
Arvada, CO 80004
(866) 811-1376
www.kristalwick.com

Pressed glass and general beading supplies:
Beadcats
PO Box 2840
Wilsonville, OR 97070-2840
(503) 625-2323
www.beadcats.com

Seed beads and general beading supplies:
Beadalon*
(866) 4-BEADALON
www.beadalon.com

Halcraft USA, Inc.*
(212) 376-1580
www.halfcraft.com

Out on a Whim
121 E. Cotati Ave.
Cotati, CA 94931
(800) 232-3111
www.whimbeads.com

Rio Grande
7500 Bluewater Rd. NW
Albuquerque, NM 87121
(800) 545-6566
www.riogrande.com

Shipwreck Beads
8560 Commerce Place Dr. NE
Lacey, WA 98516
(800) 950-4232
www.shipwreckbeads.com

Stormcloud Trading Co.
725 Snelling Ave. N
St. Paul, MN 55104
(651) 645-0343
www.beadstorm.com

Thunderbird Supply Company
1907 W Historic Rte. 66
Gallup, NM 87301
(800) 545-7968
www.thunderbirdsupply.com

Semiprecious stones and general beading supplies:
Fire Mountain Gems
One Fire Mountain Way
Grants Pass, OR 97526-2373

(800) 355-2137
www.firemountaingems.com

Sequins and buttons:
Cartwright's Sequins & Vintage Buttons
11108 N. Hwy. 348
Mountainburg, AR 72946
(479) 369-2074
www.ccartwright.com

Specialty beads and findings:
Blue Moon Beads*
www.bluemoonbeads.com

Sterling silver charms and bracelets:
Charm Factory, Inc.
PO Box 91625
Albuquerque, NM 87199
(866) 867-5266
www.charmfactory.com

Swarovski crystals and pearls:
Crystal Beads of Boston
31 Hayward St., Ste. A-1
Franklin, MA 02038
(866) 702-3237
www.crystalbeadsofboston.com

* Wholesale or distributor only.

UK SUPPLIERS
The Bead Shop
21A Tower Street
London WC2H 9NS
Tel: 020 7240 0931
www.beadworks.co.uk

Constellation Beads
The Coach House
Barningham
Richmond
North Yorkshire DL11 7DW
Tel: 01833 621094
www.constellationbeads.co.uk
(Online sales only)

Creative Beadcraft Ltd
20 Beak Street
London W1F 9RE
Tel: 020 7629 9964
www.creativebeadcraft.co.uk

Glass Beads Online
47 Broadmead
Killay
Swansea SA2 7EE

Tel: 01792 415956
www.glassbeadsonline.com
(Online sales only)

International Craft
Unit 4, The Empire Centre
Imperial Way
Watford WD24 4YH
www.internationalcraft.com

Jilly Beads Ltd
29 Hexham Road
Morecambe
Lancashire LA4 6PE
Tel: 01524 412 727
www.jillybeads.com
(Online and mail order sales only)

The Rocking Rabbit Trading Co.
7 The Green
Haddenham
CB6 3TA
Tel: 0870 606 1588
www.rockingrabbit.co.uk
(Online and mail order sales only)

The Scientific Wire Co.
18 Raven Road
London E18 1HW
Tel: 020 8505 0002
www.wires.co.uk

wirejewellery.co.uk
Faulkners Oast (East)
Tonbridge Road
Hadlow
Kent TN11 0AJ
Tel: 01732 850 727
www.wirejewellery.co.uk

Index

Acknowledgments
Grateful thanks to everyone who helped bring this book together, predominantly to
Cindy Richards and Georgina Harris at Cico Books, for giving me another opportunity of
publishing my designs. To Gloria Nicol, for her excellent photography combined with Deborah Schneebeli-Morrell's
elegant styling, to Sarah Hoggett, for her "fine toothcomb" and professional editing throughout, and to
Sara Kidd for creating the finishing touches!